On
Cloning

'. . . I think the book is a *tour de force*, and deserves to be widely read – by the critics of the author's positions as much as by the uncommitted or the already convinced.'

Richard Ashcroft, *Imperial College, London*

'Harris systematically, comprehensively and ruthlessly demolishes the opposition to cloning. The most sustained philosophical defence of cloning so far. This book will change the way society views cloning. A must for all those with an interest in applied ethics, ethics and genetics and the ethical evaluation of radical scientific developments.'

Julian Savulescu, *University of Oxford*

Praise for the series

'. . . allows a space for distinguished thinkers to write about their passions.'
The Philosophers' Magazine

'. . . deserve high praise.'
Boyd Tonkin, The Independent (UK)

'This is clearly an important series. I look forward to reading future volumes.'
Frank Kermode, author of Shakespeare's Language

'. . . both rigorous and accessible.'
Humanist News

'. . . the series looks superb.'
Quentin Skinner

'. . . an excellent and beautiful series.'
Ben Rogers, author of A.J. Ayer: A Life

'Routledge's *Thinking in Action* series is the theory junkie's answer to the eminently pocketable Penguin 60s series.'
Mute Magazine (UK)

'Routledge's new series, *Thinking in Action*, brings philosophers to our aid . . .'
The Evening Standard (UK)

'. . . a welcome new series by Routledge.'
Bulletin of Science, Technology and Society (Can)

JOHN HARRIS

On
Cloning

Routledge
Taylor & Francis Group

LONDON AND NEW YORK

First published 2004
by Routledge
11 New Fetter Lane, London EC4P 4EE

Simultaneously published in the USA and Canada
by Routledge
29 West 35th Street, New York, NY 10001

Routledge is an imprint of the Taylor & Francis Group

Typeset in Joanna MT by
RefineCatch Limited, Bungay, Suffolk
Printed and bound in Great Britain by
T.J. International Ltd, Padstow, Cornwall

British Library Cataloguing in Publication Data
A catalogue record for this book is available from the British Library

Library of Congress Cataloging in Publication Data
Harris, John, 1945–
    On cloning / John Harris. – 1st ed.
       p.   cm. – (Thinking in action)
    1. Human cloning.   2. Human cloning – Moral and ethical aspects.
    I. Title.   II. Series.
    QH442.2.H37   2004
    176 – dc22   2003026284

ISBN 0–415–31699–5 (hbk)
ISBN 0–415–31700–2 (pbk)

For
Jacob

My interest in cloning was kindled when I started thinking about cloning in the light of the birth of Louise Brown on 25 July 1978. I described the technique that eventually produced Dolly in a paper published in 1983,[1] and discussed some possible advantages of the technique in my book *The Value of Life* which was published in 1985. I am somewhat shocked to find that I have been actively thinking and writing about cloning for more than 20 years. I seem to have been one of the first philosophers to take the idea of cloning, at least as to its positive aspects, seriously, to signal the possible therapeutic advantages that it might bring and to be interested in the ethical and regulatory dilemmas it might create. Since then I have maintained the strong interest culminating in this book which aims to bring all my ideas on cloning together and also to advance the debate about the law and ethics concerning cloning in the light of developments to date.

One of the most exciting things about working in the field of the ethics of science and technology is that there is always some new discovery, or some new application for existing technologies. For this reason (and possibly also because of the essentially controversial and contested nature of ethical debate), ethical issues are never definitively resolved or closed and no 'final' word is possible. What I hope to have achieved in this book is a fairly comprehensive account of the science and ethics of cloning and of the arguments for and against the various applications of cloning that are either presently available or reasonably foreseen. I also hope that I have dispelled some of the myth and prejudice that has bedevilled cloning over the years and calmed some of the hysteria that has been all too prominent a part of public discussion of this exciting and disturbing technology.

Acknowledgements

This book owes much to many sources, some of which are human. The first source of course is Dolly, whose birth sparked a huge resurgence of interest in cloning. Although my own philosophical and ethical interest in cloning pre-dates the birth of Dolly by many years, there is no doubt that this book would not exist but for her.

More specifically I have benefited from conversations with and the stimulation of many colleagues and friends. Those who have worked on cloning, both separately and with me, and who have been a constant source of advice include Margot Brazier, Rebecca Bennett, Charles Erin, Katrien Devolder, John Robertson, Søren Holm, Simona Giordano, Inez de Beaufort, Frans Meulenberg, Louise Irving and Julian Savulescu. Of these friends Katrien Devolder and Frans Meulenberg have shared with me their extensive sources on cloning and Katrien Devolder has allowed me to use her comprehensive and invaluable bibliography which can be found via a link to the Routledge website (see bibliography for details). Louise Irving has researched international legislation and regulation and proofread the entire manuscript. Simona Giordano has also contributed more than a fair share of original ideas and practical assistance. My scientific education has been furthered by conversations with Pedro Lowenstein, Simon Winner, Alan Coleman, Susan Kimber, John Sulston,

Martin Richards, John Burn, Tom Kirkwood, George Poste, Peter Braude, Roger Pederson, Steven Minger, Susan Pickering, Anne McLaren, Peter Lachmann and William B. Provine. I must thank Joanna Quinlan for work on the sources and bibliography. Peter Lipton and Richard Ashcroft read the manuscript on behalf of Routledge and I have benefited from their detailed comments.

Particular points of legal and regulatory advice have been gratefully received from, Carlos Romeo-Casabona, Ludger Honnefelder, Dave Booton, Kirsty Keywood, Ruth Deech and Margot Brazier. I thank Daniela-Ecaterina Cutas for compiling the index.

Work on this book was supported by a project grant from the European Commission for the project 'EUROSTEM' under its 'Quality of Life and Management of Living Resources' Programme, 2002. I must also acknowledge support from another project: *Science, Fiction and Science-fiction – the role of literature in public debates on medical ethical issues and in the medical education* led by Inez de Beaufort under the same European Commission programme. My colleagues at the School of Law, University of Manchester, kindly agreed to grant me a semester of study leave (only my second such semester in 30 years of teaching) to allow some extra opportunity to work on this and other projects. Finally, Tony Bruce, my editor at Routledge, was always hugely supportive.

One

The birth of Dolly, the world-famous cloned sheep, triggered the most extraordinary re-awakening of interest in, and concern about, cloning and indeed about scientific and technological innovation and its regulation and control. She has fuelled debate in a number of fora: genetic and scientific, political and moral, journalistic and literary. She has also given birth to a number of myths, not least among which is the myth that she represents a danger to humanity, the human gene pool, genetic diversity, the ecosystem, the world as we know it, and to the survival of the human species. Cloning is a technology and indeed a subject that has gripped the public imagination. The mere mention of the word 'cloning' sells books, films and even newspapers. Cloning also raises blood pressure and causes panic in equal measure and to an extent unprecedented in recent science.

More importantly perhaps, Dolly, or the technology by which she was created, raises many different sorts of important questions for us all. Some of these questions concern human rights and how we are to understand the idea of respect for these rights and for human dignity. Others direct our attention to the ways in which we attempt to pursue scientific research and bring that research to the point at which it is safe to offer therapies or products to the public. Other questions make us reflect upon the ways in which we attempt to regulate or control both science and indeed personal and public access to the fruits of science. Finally there are fundamental issues about the standards of evidence and argument that we do or should demand before we attempt to control or limit human freedom. All of these questions and issues are of the first importance and all of them come together and are engaged when we consider the ethical, legal and regulatory issues presented by human cloning. It is these questions and issues that are the subject and object of this book.

Before investigating these issues, however, we should be clear about just what cloning means and how it came about.

WHAT IS CLONING?[1]

Cloning refers to asexual reproduction, reproduction without 'fertilisation'. A cloned individual (clone from the Greek *Klon*, 'twig', 'slip') may result from two different processes: (1) Embryo splitting: this sometimes gives rise to monozygotic twins but can also result in identical triplets or even quadruplets.[2] (2) Cell Nuclear Replacement (CNR) or Cell Nuclear Transfer (CNT). This was the procedure that produced Dolly. CNR involves two cells: a recipient, which is generally an egg (oocyte), and a donor cell. Early experiments mainly made use of embryonic cells, which were expected to behave similarly to the cells of a fertilised egg, in order to promote normal development after the nuclear replacement. In more recent experiments, the donor cells were taken from either fetal or adult tissues. The nucleus of the donor cell is introduced into the egg (either by cell fusion or by injection). With appropriate stimulation – electric pulses or exposure to chemicals – the egg is induced to develop. The embryo thus created may be implanted in a viable womb, and then develops in the normal way to term, although the failure rate has so far been high.

It is clear then that cloning did not start with the birth of Dolly nor yet did artificially produced clones start with the birth of Dolly. The first type of cloning was, as we have noted, the creation, through sexual reproduction, of so-called identical (monozygotic) twins. These sorts of clones have always been with us and, confining ourselves to humans for the moment, humankind has a vast, and on the whole successful, experience with them.

So, the first type of deliberate cloning we must consider is 'embryo splitting' which results in monozygotic twins.

EMBRYO SPLITTING

When identical twins occur in nature they result from the splitting of the early embryo in utero and the resulting twins have identical genomes. This process can be mimicked in the laboratory and in vitro embryos can be deliberately split creating matching siblings.

This process itself has a number of ethically puzzling if not problematic features. If you have a pre-implantation embryo in the early stages of development where all cells are what is called 'toti-potential' (that is where all cells could become any part of the resulting individual or indeed could develop into a whole new individual) and if you take this early cell mass and split it, let us say into four clumps of cells, each one of these four clumps constitutes a new embryo which is viable and could be implanted with the hope of successful development into adulthood. Each clump is the clone or identical 'twin' of any of the others and comes into being not through conception but because of the division of the early cell mass. Moreover, these four clumps can be recombined into one embryo again. This creates a situation where, without the destruction of a single human cell, one human life, if that is what it is, can be split into four and can be recombined again into one. Did 'life' in such a case begin as an individual, become four individuals and then turn into a singleton again? We should note that whatever our answer to this question, all this occurred without the creation of extra matter and without the destruction of a single cell. Those who think that ensoulment takes place at conception have an interesting problem to account for the splitting of one soul into four, and for the destruction of three souls when the four embryos are recombined into one, and to account for (and resolve the ethics of) the destruction of three individuals, without a single human cell being removed or killed. These possibilities should, perhaps, give us pause in attributing a beginning of morally important life to a point like conception.[3]

Monozygotic twins, whether created as the natural result of sexual reproduction or by splitting pre-implantation embryos in the laboratory, are the most closely matched clones possible. If such twins share the same uterine environment then not only do they have in common all their DNA, including the mitochondrial DNA present in the egg, but they will also share the other maternal and probably the other important environmental influences that shape us all (see below).

Incidentally, the process of embryo splitting reveals as illusory one oft-repeated fear concerning cloning. The fear that once a technology exists it will inevitably be used, and that this alleged 'fact' coupled with the attractiveness of cloning will lead inevitably to its widespread use. The technique of embryo splitting has been known and usable for many years and yet there has neither been pressure to adopt this deliberately to produce clones nor any apparent regret that this has not been done.

Of course it may be said that clones produced by embryo splitting are not diachronous in the way that clones using CNR (see below) would be. They would not be identical siblings separated in time of birth. However, again the technique for achieving this has also been available virtually since IVF began more than 20 years ago. Once split, one of the two (or four) siblings can be frozen and implanted many years after the first 'batch' have been born. Again there seems to have been no pressure to produce clones by this, now long established, route.[4]

NUCLEAR REPLACEMENT

We have noted the way in which cell nuclear replacement can be used to create clones like Dolly. A first feature of this process to note is that it is false to think that the clone produced by CNR is the genetic child of the nucleus donor. It is not. The clone is the twin brother or sister of the nucleus donor and the genetic offspring of the nucleus donor's own parents. Thus this type of cloned individual is, and always must be, the genetic child of two separate genotypes, of two genetically different individuals, however often it is cloned or re-cloned. The presence of the mitochondrial genome of a third individual means that the genetic inheritance of clones is in fact richer than that of other individuals, richer in the sense of being more variously derived.[5] This can be important if the nucleus donor is subject to mitochondria diseases inherited from his or her mother and wants a child genetically related to her that will be free of these diseases.

The first experiments on cloning techniques were made in 1928 with a salamander embryo[6] and continued by Jacques

Loeb and Hans Spemann who worked on frogs and sea-urchins in Germany in 1938. By the early 1930s the idea of cloning was already part of the public consciousness, so much so that it could feature in Aldous Huxley's novel *Brave New World*, first published in 1932.[7] In 1952 the first cloned tadpoles appeared.[8] Experiments on mice and cattle and sheep began[9] and the first cloned creature produced from fetal and adult mammalian cells was reported from an Edinburgh based group in *Nature* on 27 February 1997 (Wilmut, I. et al. 1997). 'Dolly', now the world's most famous sheep, caused a sensation, not least because it had come to be assumed that cloning large animals like sheep or humans would not be possible. Dolly's birth re-awakened the huge popular interest in human attempts to create life by design rather than by a random combination of genes. Cloning has become one of the most hotly debated and least well-understood phenomena in contemporary science, let alone contemporary bioethics.

POTENTIAL APPLICATIONS[10]
Cell therapy

One of the potential therapeutic applications of CNR is in the field of cell therapy. Stem cells are cells that have the capacity to give rise to different cell types and therefore to develop into different bodily tissues and organs. Embryonic stem cells (ESC) have the capacity to differentiate in *all* human tissues (except for extra-embryonic tissues, such as the placenta and umbilical cord – normally ESC are called 'pluripotent' in virtue of this 'plural potentiality'. ('Totipotential' is the power to develop into any part of the organism, including the whole organism, and is a power possessed, for example, by the zygote – the newly fertilised egg). Thus it is hoped that ESC can be used to repair or rebuild any damaged or malfunctioning bodily system if introduced into the appropriate part of the body. This is how it might work. A zygote would be created through CNR, and the nucleus of a cell taken from the person who needs the transplantation would be used. The zygote would be grown to the blastocyst stage. At this stage the embryo presents itself as a hollow cavity containing ESC. These may be easily harvested and cultured in *vitro*, and made limitlessly available, given their capacity to replicate. ESC thus created would be particularly suitable for transplantation, as these cells are genetically 'matched' to the recipient's using cells created from the nucleus of a cell taken from the recipient herself.

It is sometimes argued that 'individual' treatment, such as described above, is unrealistic due to the high costs of the procedure and to the need for a continuing supply of human eggs for CNR. A less speculative therapeutic application than the creation of compatible tissues on an individual basis is thought to be the creation of ESC banks through CNR. From these banks, cells and tissues that appear more compatible with the patient's would be selected.

If the potential of CNR for cell therapy is realised and fully utilised, the benefits for humanity would be great.[11] Among the diseases that might be treatable in this way are Alzheimer's disease, spinal cord injuries, multiple sclerosis, stroke, Parkinson's disease, diabetes, cancer, osteoporosis, muscular dystrophy.[12] It is important to stress that if CNR could be used to create compatible closely matching tissues, this would overcome two major problems: (1) shortage of tissues, and (2) immunological rejection. The recipient's immune system normally recognises the transplanted tissue (or organ) as 'foreign' and rejects it. Immuno-suppressant drugs are used to minimise the risk of rejection, but they are not always effective and must normally be taken for the entire duration of the patient's life, thus leaving them vulnerable to infections.

Creation of compatible organs

The creation of compatible organs through CNR is one of the major potential therapeutic applications of the technique, although it is currently regarded as highly speculative. Again the capacity of stem cells to form any part of the human organism would be harnessed to create 'tailor-made' organs, which, because they are formed from cells, which are clones of the intended recipient, would be compatible and immune from the body's normal mechanisms for rejecting 'foreign' tissue. The procedure would be the same described above, up to the point of harvesting ESC. Ideally, ESC might be induced to differentiate in the laboratory, that is, to specialise into specific types of cells, and then grown until a full organ could be available for transplant. In a future scenario, this procedure would obviate the major problem of shortage of organs, as people in need of an organ could have 'their own' spare organs created by this means, and the problem of immunological rejection would be solved by cloning the cells used.

Treatment of mitochondrial disease

Mitochondria are energy-producing structures present in the cytoplasm of every cell. Mitochondria are not transferred from the male gametes during fertilisation, and only the mitochondria present in the oocyte will be inherited by the embryo. Mitochondria are thus only inherited from the mother. Mitochondrial alterations are relatively rare but result in very serious diseases. Through CNR, it would be possible to replace the mother's mitochondrial DNA with that of a healthy donor. This technique would involve a donated oocyte, from which the nucleus would be removed; and the nucleus of the mother's egg (the nucleus of the cell does not contain cytoplasm), which would be introduced in the denucleated donated healthy oocyte. With this technique a 'new' oocyte would be created, with the healthy nucleus of the mother and the healthy cytoplasm of a donor. This 'new' oocyte would preserve the vast majority of DNA of the mother, plus a small amount of DNA (mitochondrial DNA) from the donor. The 'new' oocyte would then be ready for *in vitro* fertilisation with the father's sperm.

Differently from the CNR technique discussed above, the embryo in this case would preserve the genetic material of two individuals (the mother, who gives the nucleus, and the father), and in addition it would have a small amount of DNA from a third person (mitochondrial DNA from the donor of the oocyte). The embryo, therefore, will not possess an 'identical copy' of the genome of any of the three persons involved in the process.

Creation of embryos for research

The feasibility of these procedures rests on embryo research. Embryos may be made available by *in vitro* fertilisation (IVF) clinics (supernumerary or spare embryos), and they may also be created specifically for research purposes through either IVF or CNR. The international community is divided on the ethics of creating embryos for research purposes. It is often considered more ethical to use spare embryos from IVF treatment. However, CNR would be necessary to investigate the behaviour of adult stem cells and also to assess whether tissue that is compatible with an individual recipient may be created.

Understanding processes of differentiation, de-differentiation and re-differentiation of stem cells

Until recently it was believed that the process of differentiation of stem cells was irreversible, that is that a cell, once specialised, could not be 'brought back' to its unspecialised stage. Experiments on animals have instead demonstrated that it is possible, in some cases, to de-differentiate specialised adult cells. Adult cells of a specific type may de-differentiate to pluripotency and then specialise again to generate a different cell type from the one they were originally programmed to generate; or a cell may change into a different cell type without going through the de-differentiation phase (this process is sometimes called 'transdifferentiation').[13] Once these processes are fully understood, it may be possible to produce tissues and organs that are compatible with the recipient (given that the cells utilised in the therapy would belong to them), without creating embryos and harvesting ESC. This would resolve problems of shortage of organs, problems of immunological rejection and would satisfy those who believe that creating and killing embryos is unethical. However, the vast majority of the scientific community believes that research on adult stem cells does not currently make research on ESC redundant, and CNR research is held to be the only realistic means fully to understand the processes of differentiation and de-differentiation of human cells.

Reproduction

In theory CNR could be utilised for reproductive purposes. In this case the embryo created through CNR would be implanted in a viable womb and grown to term. CNR would have in this case similar potential applications to IVF. It would enable single parents or gay couples to have children genetically related to themselves, without unwanted DNA, gender selection in cases of gender-related diseases, and infertile couples to have children without using donor gametes.

These potential applications of CNR are currently regarded as highly speculative by the scientific community. Given the technical problems discussed below, the reproductive use of CNR would require a degree of experimentation on human beings that is currently regarded as unacceptable, and this is likely to mean that CNR will be not regarded, at least for the foreseeable future, as a viable method of reproduction.

Other applications

CNR could be used to clone genetically modified animals, a prospect that may offer important benefits for human health. The idea is to create animals whose milk, for example, might become a means to administer medicines or proteins or even vaccinations, and then clone these animals so that their genetic characteristics are not lost during reproduction.

TECHNICAL PROBLEMS

Before CNR can be successfully employed in any of the applications described above, the following technical problems (as well as those of the cost of such procedures) must be resolved.

Scarcity of oocytes: Oocytes are a very scarce resource much in demand for treatment of infertility: currently 12–13 oocytes are needed to create one embryo through CNR.

Genetic makeup: The embryo created by CNR would not be genetically identical to the nucleus's donor, as it will inherit the mitochondrial DNA from the oocyte donor. The implications of this in terms of immunological compatibility are unknown. This may also have unknown implications if CNR is utilised in the treatment of mitochondrial disease.

Development of cloned stem cells: It is unclear whether stem cells produced by CNR would develop and age in the same way as stem cells produced by 'natural' or artificial fertilisation.[14]

Behaviour of cloned SC: It is unknown whether, once the stem cells derived by CNR were transplanted into the recipient, they would behave normally, whether they would be able to function normally and to integrate with the other cells in a normal way. The main risk is that they may give rise to tumours.[15]

Long-term safety: The long-term safety of transplants of tissues derived by CNR is unknown.

Purity of the tissues: At present almost all stem cells have been grown on a culture medium which is derived from animals. This would present dangers if the cells were used in therapy for humans. Until a safe culture medium for growing stem cells is proved, human therapeutic applications will be for the most part too dangerous to contemplate.

Illnesses of the donor: the somatic cell from which the nucleus is taken may carry the genetic defect for which the person is being treated, although genetic engineering could in theory help to overcome this problem.

Large-scale production: There are the challenges of production of stem cells by CNR on a large scale.

Fetal abnormalities: with regard to the reproductive use of CNR, a high risk of abnormalities in fetuses and high premature mortality is registered.

These problems give us reasons to be cautious, but many similar unknown outcomes attend the introduction of almost every new technology. If we never embarked on a new therapy or technology until all the possible consequences were clear and certain there would never be any new technologies at all. Elsewhere my colleague Søren Holm and I have set out a detailed rejection of the precautionary principle.[16] Here I will simply summarise some of our conclusions that are relevant to an assessment of just how much unknown factors should influence our reception or rejection of a new technology.

The so-called 'precautionary principle' inexorably requires science to be ultra conservative and irrationally cautious and societies to reject a wide spectrum of possible benefits from scientific advance and technological change. Thus, unlike many moral principles that have found their way into the field of social policy and have found expression in contemporary protocols, regulations, and even treaties and laws, the precaution has immense potential for good or ill.

What does the precautionary principle require?

Proponents of the 'precautionary principle' (PP) from more than 30 universities and government agencies issued the Wingspread Statement on the precautionary principle in 1998, which explains the PP as follows:

> When an activity raises threats of harm to human health or the environment precautionary measures should be taken even if some cause and effect relationships are not fully established scientifically. In this context the proponent of an activity, rather than the public, should bear the burden of proof.[17]

One way of understanding the PP would be as a principle of

rational choice. This would involve the claim that in circumstances in which decisions must be made and where the PP could be applied, it would be rational to apply it and follow the conclusions drawn from such an application. There are, however, some problems with the PP as a principle of rational choice.

The first problem is inherent in the specification of the harm which is to be avoided by precautionary measures. Often harms are thought of as to be avoided in proportion to a combination of irreversibility and seriousness. But the mere fact that a harm is irreversible does not entail that it is serious in any way. If somebody without permission were to place a 1 mm long ineradicable scar on the sole of someone else's foot, the 'victim' would have been irreversibly harmed, but it would be difficult to claim that she had been seriously harmed. It is also the case that many harms are irreversible, without thereby being irremediable. If you block your neighbour's driveway so that he has to take a taxi to work on a specific day, the harm you have done is irreversible (because time is irreversible), but it is not irremediable. That a harm is irreversible does therefore not in itself tell us anything about the weight we should give to this harm in our rational decision-making, and mere irreversibility of harm can therefore not justify invoking precautionary measures.

Similarly the mere fact that a harm is serious is also, in some cases, insufficient to show that it must be prevented, for example when the harm though serious is fully reversible or fully remediable.

Modified precaution

If the PP is valid at all it can therefore only be valid in cases where there is risk of a harm which is 'Serious *and* both irreversible and irremediable'. This formulation of the principle was devised by John Harris and Søren Holm:

> When an activity raises threats of serious and both irreversible and irremediable harm to human health or the environment precautionary measures which effectively prevent the possibility of harm (e.g. moratorium, prohibition, etc.) shall be taken even if the causal link between the activity and the possible harm has not been proven or the causal link is weak and the harm is unlikely to occur.

In the context of human health we need to know whether it is sufficient and/or necessary for a harm to be 'serious' that it will seriously affect the health of one person, or whether it is sufficient and/or necessary that the aggregate harm to a group of people adds up to being 'serious', or perhaps some combination of these options. Depending on what definition of 'serious' one chooses, very different activities are marked out as falling under the PP (i.e. as being PP-serious).

If, on the one hand, a serious effect on one person is sufficient for something to be PP-serious then the PP entails that the inventor of apple pie should have applied the PP, and let the first pie be the last, since there have been people who have choked to death on apple pie. If, contrariwise, a combined serious effect on health is sufficient for PP-seriousness, then the PP clearly rules out any further procreative acts resulting in pregnancy and childbirth since these are highly dangerous to both mother and child. And if finally it is sufficient that a harm is either serious at the individual or at the group level then the PP seems to rule out both motherhood and apple pie.[18] But here we are not simply talking about legislating against motherhood and apple pie, attractive as that might seem. We are talking about being so cautious as to deprive people of the possibility of therapies for crippling and lethal conditions and standing by while victims mount up year on year.

The bottom line is that when precaution is invoked there are always two different and equally important reasons for caution and ways to be cautious. On the one hand there are the possible dangers of the new technology, therapy or procedure; on the other there are the dangers of delaying the introduction of these, by hypothesis, life-extending or danger-averting therapies or technologies. We always have to be cognisant of the harm a new technology might do, and set against that the harm that will continue to occur unless it is introduced to stem that harm. This is often an impossibly difficult calculation to make and equally often there will be no hard evidence one way or the other. The precautionary principle urges us to give more weight to the dangers inherent in the new technology than to the avoidance of the dangers that its introduction will achieve. This is irrational. What we must do is give most weight to the most serious and most probable dangers, and unless we know which these are we have no reason to invoke the precautionary principle.

WHY, DESPITE THE PROBLEMS, WE MUST PURSUE RESEARCH WHICH USES CNR

It is important that the reasons to pursue CNR (so called 'therapeutic cloning') are not lost in the detail; nor because of the technical problems, nor the unresolved issues, nor the minutiae of the precautionary principle. To give 'colour' to the rather dispassionate discussion of possible uses let me record two passages from recent scientific papers.

Roger A. Pedersen[19] noted recently:

Research on embryonic stem cells will ultimately lead to techniques for generating cells that can be employed in therapies, not just for heart attacks, but for many conditions in which tissue is damaged.

If it were possible to control the differentiation of human embryonic stem cells in culture the resulting cells could potentially help repair damage caused by congestive heart failure, Parkinson's Disease, diabetes and other afflictions. They could prove especially valuable for treating conditions affecting the heart and the islets of the pancreas, which retain few or no stem cells in an adult and so cannot renew themselves naturally.

One therapeutic use of stem cells that should be highlighted, because of the large numbers of people who might benefit, is in the case of skin grafts, as Mooney and Mikos have emphasised:

The need for skin is acute: every year six hundred thousand Americans suffer from diabetic ulcers, which are particularly difficult to heal; another six hundred thousand have skin removed to treat skin cancer; and between ten thousand and fifteen thousand undergo skin grafts to treat severe burns.

The next tissue to be widely used in humans will most likely be cartilage for orthopedic, craniofacial and urological applications. Currently available cartilage is insufficient for the half a million operations annually in the US that repair damaged joints and for the additional twenty-eight thousand face and head reconstructive surgeries.[20]

Having reminded ourselves of some of the research and therapeutic possibilities, it is important to remind ourselves of the moral reasons we have to pursue these research and therapeutic possibilities. 'Research' always sounds such an abstract and even vainglorious objective when set against passionate feelings of fear or distaste. We need to remind ourselves of the human benefits that stem from research and the human costs of not pursuing research.

Stem cells for organ and tissue transplant

It is difficult to estimate how many people might benefit from the products of stem cell research should it be permitted and prove fruitful. Perhaps the remotest of the likely products of stem cell research would be tailor-made human organs, but at least in this field we have some reliable data on the numbers of human lives that wait on the development of better ways of coping with their need to replace or repair damaged organs.

> 'In the world as a whole there are an estimated 700,000 patients on dialysis. . . . In India alone 100,000 new patients present with kidney failure each year' (few if any of whom are on dialysis and only 3,000 of whom will receive transplants). Almost '3 million Americans suffer from congestive heart failure . . . deaths related to this condition are estimated at 250,000 each year . . . 27,000 patients die annually from liver disease. . . . In Western Europe as a whole 40,000 patients await a kidney but only . . . 10,000 kidneys' become available. Nobody knows how many people fail to make it onto the waiting lists and so disappear from the statistics.[21]

While the days of genetically modified tailor-made organs are still very far off, compatible organs may one day supply many of the needs for tissue repair and replacement releasing more donor organs to meet transplant needs which cannot be met in other ways.

Most sources agree that the most proximate use of human

ES cell therapy would be for Parkinson's disease. Parkinson's disease 'is a common neurological disease' the prevalence of which increases with age. 'The overall prevalence (per 100 population in persons 65 years of age and older'[22]) is 1.8. Parkinson's has a disastrous effect on quality of life. Another source speculates that 'the true prevalence of idiopathic Parkinson's disease in London may be around 200 per 100,000'.[23] In the United Kingdom around 120,000 individuals have Parkinson's,[24] and it is estimated that Parkinson's disease affects between one and one-and-a-half million Americans.[25] Untold human misery and suffering could be stemmed if Parkinson's disease became treatable.

If Roger Pedersen's hopes for stem cell therapy are realised and treatments become available for congestive heart failure, diabetes and other afflictions and if, as many believe, tailor-made transplant organs will eventually be possible, then literally millions of people worldwide will be treated using stem cell therapy.

When a possible new therapy holds out promise of dramatic cures we should of course be cautious, if only to dampen false hopes of an early treatment; but equally we should, for the sake of all those awaiting therapy, pursue the research that might lead to therapy with all vigour. To fail to do so would be to deny people who might benefit the possibility of therapy. This creates a positive moral duty to pursue this research.

THE REACTION TO THE BIRTH OF DOLLY

When Dolly's birth was reported in *Nature* on 27 February 1997[26] the reaction was nothing short of hysterical. The then President of the United States, Bill Clinton, called immediately for an investigation into the ethics of such procedures[27] and announced a moratorium on public spending on human cloning. President Clinton said: 'There is virtually unanimous consensus in the scientific and medical communities that attempting to use these cloning techniques to actually clone a human being is untested and unsafe and morally unacceptable'.[28] George W. Bush, has repeated this ritual genuflexion in the direction of hostility to cloning. 'I strongly oppose human cloning, as do most Americans. We recoil at the idea of growing human beings for spare parts, or creating life for our convenience.'[29]

Members of the European Parliament (MEPs) demanded that each EU member 'enact binding legislation prohibiting all research on human cloning and providing criminal sanctions for any breach'.[30] The European Parliament rushed through a resolution on cloning, the preamble of which asserted, (Paragraph B):

[T]he cloning of human beings . . . cannot under any circumstances be justified or tolerated by any society, because it is a serious violation of fundamental human rights and is contrary to the principle of equality of human beings as it permits a eugenic and racist selection of the human race, it offends against human dignity and it requires experimentation on humans

And which went on to claim that, (Clause 1):

each individual has a right to his or her own genetic identity and that human cloning is, and must continue to be, prohibited.[31]

Following swiftly on the tail of the European Parliament, the 'Additional Protocol to the Convention for the Protection of Human Rights and Dignity of the Human Being with regard

to the Application of Biology and Medicine, on the Prohibition of Cloning Human Beings' of the Council Of Europe
was promulgated in Paris, 1 December 1998, again, one may
think, in some haste if not panic following the birth of Dolly.
It states:

> . . . Considering the purpose of the Convention on Human
> Rights and Biomedicine, in particular the principle mentioned
> in Article 1 aiming to protect the dignity and identity of all
> human beings, Have agreed as follows:

Article 1

> 1. Any intervention seeking to create a human being genetic-
>   ally identical to another human being, whether living or
>   dead, is prohibited.
> 2. For the purpose of this article, the term human being 'gen-
>   etically identical' to another human being means a human
>   being sharing with another the same nuclear gene set.

These statements are almost entirely devoid of argument and
rationale. There are vague references to 'human rights' or
'dignity' or the importance of 'genetic identity' with little or
no attempt to explain what these principles are, or to indicate
how they might apply to cloning.

The United Kingdom Government, for example, states
proudly 'The Government has made its position on reproductive cloning absolutely clear on a number of occasions. On
26 June 1997, the then Minister for Public Health stated in
response to a Question in Parliament:

> 'We regard the deliberate cloning of human beings as
> ethically unacceptable. Under United Kingdom Law, cloning
> of individual humans cannot take place whatever the origin of

the material and whatever the technique is used'. This remains the Government's position[32]

The United Kingdom Government has now outlawed human reproductive cloning in the hastily drafted Human Reproductive Cloning Act 2001. This hostility to cloning follows closely the pronouncements of many other bodies both in Europe and across the world.

These statements on human cloning by ethics commissions and parliaments and world leaders contain claims about the wickedness of cloning. The claims are asserted as if they are either self-evident, or as if the arguments and evidence supporting them are so well known and clearly established that citation is superfluous. Are there any plausible arguments and is there any evidence that might sustain these claims? What should our response to human cloning be? What would a responsible legislative and regulatory response to cloning look like? How can the welfare of possible cloned children be protected? How can scientific research which uses cloning technology be responsibly and ethically pursued? This book sets out to answer these questions.

However, there is an initial puzzle to be considered. Why has cloning exercised such a grip on the imagination? Why has it proved so fascinating and so seductive? There have been a very large number of books and newspaper articles devoted to the science and ethics of cloning and a substantial popular literature and many major films with cloning as their theme. Some of the most important of these are listed in the Bibliography.

WHY HAS CLONING PROVED SUCH A SEDUCTIVE IDEA?

In part, the hysterical reaction to cloning that we have noted is a testimony to its fascination and to the, perhaps disproportionate, importance it has been given. But why the hysteria, why the importance and why the fascination?

There are obviously no easy or definitive answers to such questions; but speculation, like gossip, is fun and may be instructive. I claim no special expertise nor insight into these questions, but before we turn to the philosophical analysis of the arguments and issues raised by cloning it is worth trying to gain some understanding of why so much heat and so little light has been generated by cloning and reactions to the very idea of cloning. Certainly I have tried to arrive at some idea of why cloning has so gripped the popular imagination – these are my initial conclusions.

Many of the things that fascinate humans seem to combine in cloning. I say 'seem' because, as we shall see, many of these arresting ideas are not involved in cloning at all. Let's start with what seems to be true of cloning.

1. Blood will out!

'Blood will out!' is an old, and rather distasteful, expression of a commitment to the importance of close family relations, breeding and heredity. Genes are the contemporary replacement for the idea of the contribution of 'blood' and 'blood relationships' between humans. So my interest in my blood relations, my blood kin, is fulfilled 100% in anyone with whom I share all my genes – my clone! Of course this begs certain questions about the basis of kinship and emphasises the significance of genetic relatedness, which may be problematic for many reasons. Despite the pervasive interest in 'blood' or genetic relatedness there is a deep confusion at the heart of the idea. This is because all human beings and indeed all organic life is strongly genetically related. A mother shares 99.95% of her genes with her daughter, but she shares

99.90% of her genes with any randomly selected person on the planet. We all share over 90% of our genes with chimpanzees and 50% with bananas! Bananas are thus our 'blood' relations (bloodless though they may be). And of course if I am interested in who my blood relations are, I am also likely to be interested in begetting some blood relations, which brings us neatly to the genetic imperative.

2. The genetic imperative

The so-called 'genetic imperative' is obviously also related to this idea of blood relationships. The idea of spreading our blood and hence our genes, and securing the survival in a sense, of parts of ourselves, is powerful indeed. Again, the power is at its maximum when we believe we might pass on not simply *part* of ourselves but *all* of ourselves. Perhaps because we now know that we share such a high percentage of our genes with strangers, the idea of gaining that extra fraction of a percentage in common with others is part of the attraction of cloning. This idea of a genetic imperative is part of a, not altogether unproblematic, interest in who our children and who our parents are or were. In part of course this is bound up with ideas about sexual fidelity within relationships and within marriage, sexual jealousy and also inheritance; but it has also become linked with more vague ideas about genetic identity and the alleged importance of knowing one's genetic origins. These ideas also are more than a little problematic.

For example, there are significant non-paternity rates in the United Kingdom and other countries. Non-paternity refers to births where the children of the family are not in fact genetically related to the person they believe to be their father (and who usually believes that he is their genetic father).

Non-paternity rates are quoted with wildly differing values (from less than 1% to more than 30%). A modest, and probably reliable, figure is 2%.[33] However even at a modest rate of 2% non-paternity rates in the United Kingdom account for over 12,000 births registered annually to men who are not in fact the genetic father.[34] Thus if there is such a thing as a 'need for children to know their genetic background and true identity', then on the grounds of numbers alone we should start with normal families. This might imply an obligation for paternity testing in all families! The mischief and disruption this would cause is clearly incalculable. What price then a so-called 'need to know one's genetic origin'! I do not believe there is any such thing but if there is, it is doubtful that the arguments which might sustain it are such as to outweigh the rights of privacy of sperm donors still less the rights to protection of the privacy of family life. So while we have an undoubted interest in the identity of our genetic relations, the legitimacy of satisfying that interest is problematic. The fascination of cloning then partly stems from our interest in those to whom we are genetically related. This interest has many dimensions and the degree of interest is often proportional to the degree of relatedness, hence maximal interest in clones and cloning.

3. Immortality

Immortality is a seductive idea. Not only do we wish to avoid death and oblivion, but many of us also want to live forever, to miss nothing and enjoy everything. If we cannot ourselves live forever, then expedients which seem to offer something closely related to immortality often seem attractive. Some people for example have resorted to cryopreservation, to freezing their bodies when terminally ill in the hope that they can be thawed out in the future when effective treatments become available for their illness. If our genes can survive, inhabiting so to speak a facsimile of ourselves, then perhaps this is the next best thing, to clone ourselves if not to duplicate ourselves! Cloning appears to some as a way of making a photo or Xerox copy of ourselves that would replace us and survive to clone/copy itself again indefinitely down the ages.[35]

4. Playing God!

Many aspire to the status of gods, and playing God, so far from being a discreditable activity, as it is also often represented to be, is in fact something that seems to be a constant temptation, and for many an inevitable part of life. One of God's great accomplishments, so far as certain believing humans go, is creating creatures in his own image. Cloning allows anyone to create a creature in his or her own image – to play God in one important dimension of the fullest sense of the term. Thus the creation of a creature quite literally in our image and to our pattern and 'blueprint' is a heady prospect, which allows us mortals to partake of the attributes of God. We can not only manufacture life to our design but in our own personal image.

5. Mimesis

The ideas we have already reviewed are obviously intimately related – dimensions of the same idea, the same craving or hope. Linked to these more tenuously is the idea of and fascination for likenesses, copies, facsimiles, duplicates and reproductions; in short for *mimesis*. We seek mirror images, portraits, photographs, silhouettes, profiles; in art verisimilitude has always been popular; figurative painting, drawing and sculpture, art that looks like the world, that 'holds a mirror up to nature', feels perennial, eternal, in a way that abstraction seems, and perhaps is, transient.

6. The re-creation of a particular, often a famous, character

In many of the fictional treatments of cloning the idea of re-creating or preserving a particular historical character is the central idea. Famously *The Boys from Brazil* involved the idea of re-creating Hitler from his DNA; and Michael Crighton's brilliant *Jurassic Park* involved the re-creation of particular species of dinosaurs, with the most famous historical character being *Tyrannosaurus Rex*. The idea that we might see again and even meet a famous or infamous person from the past is of enduring interest, combining as it does a sort of hero-worship with fantasies about how we would ourselves react to the encounter or how the historical character would cope in today's world, or how they might re-create the glories with which they are associated. In some ways this idea is a sort of reverse time travel; instead of ourselves returning to some past era, important individual features of that era are brought forward to us.

7. Reproduction

It is not for nothing that we speak of sexual *reproduction*. We reproduce, and *a fortiori*, we reproduce ourselves. That is to say, we copy ourselves; we produce copies; that is what reproduction is. Visual art – drawing, painting, sculpture and, for that matter, the literary arts – poetry, plays, essays, novels and so on, were also all about mimesis and the production of reality. Likewise, cartography, plans, instructions, blue-prints, elevations, projections, models, cartoons, and the like – all ways of copying, reproducing nature. The fascination of cloning embodies in a dramatic and complete form this urge and desire to reproduce 'things' and ourselves. To clone oneself is to be at once a consummate artist and a divine creator. If ordinary sexual reproduction is to reproduce oneself – like God, to create creatures in our image but not exactly like us – then cloning is to go a step further, to create creatures thought to be exactly in our image.

8. Mechanical reproduction

Next to art and to cloning, industrial production partakes of the power of creation. And cloning combines both art and industry, artifice and technology. In industrial production, very often the creation of a prototype is followed by the, in principle endless, production of copies of the prototype. The magic of the paper chain, in which a string of 'people' are created out of cut paper, is allied to the limitless fecundity of industrial production; armies of identical individuals, copies of some desired or admired prototype. This idea of limitless copies of a prototype is of course a long way off and requires much more than cloning technology. The number of copies obtainable by human reproductive cloning is limited for the foreseeable future by many features, not least the number of willing or coercible gestating mothers.

9. Predictability and control

Although cloning appears to offer the prospect of creating limitless numbers of a desired prototype, and hence the pro-spect of 'armies' of willing and directable servants, soldiers or slaves, cloning really offers nothing new here. For one thing there is no evidence that the genotype of a slave is a slavish genotype,[36] nor that the genes of a warrior create brave fighters. Moreover, cloning offers little new or more in the way of efficiency to the megalomaniac. Dictators have always been able to rape women and force them to have their babies. We know of rulers who had harems of thousands of women, but they were not conspicuously successful when compared to others of more modest appetite.

10. The mad scientist

The idea of the mad scientist creating monsters and men, and sometimes both, is an enduring image. One of the earliest and most famous examples is of course Mary Shelley's *Frankenstein*; but Aldous Huxley's *Brave New World* and Michael Crighton's *Jurassic Park* are other notable examples. Quite why people like, or like to be terrified by, the idea of mad or megalomaniacal scientists I am not sure. It might be the idea of the perversion or fallibility of brilliance, it might be that as scientists are supposed to be 'unworldly' and perhaps also 'lacking in common sense', they are obvious candidates for the sort of disastrous mistakes that make good 'copy' in journalistic terms. In any event since scientists are and will for the foreseeable future be the only begetters of cloning technology, if not of clones, they, and their supposed weaknesses of character, help to add to the fascination of cloning.

11. The lottery of sexual reproduction

Another attraction of cloning, which is perhaps of some enduring importance, is that it removes the random lottery of sexual reproduction in which almost anything could happen, including the production of monsters or magi. Cloning combines genetic predictability with the advantages of a tried and tested genome, a genome we know that has stood the test of time and in all probability will do so again. This consequence of the refinement of cloning technology is one of the few that offers one of the real potential benefits of reproductive cloning, the opportunity to eliminate or more realistically minimise the chances of a range of errors or undesirable traits being produced by the essentially random 'gamble' of sexual reproduction.

12. A good start in life

The fact that cloning might enable us to give our children a good genetic start in life constitutes a strong argument in favour of reproductive cloning. It is not clear why people object to this prospect. We already try to give our children the best start in life now, by creating the best conditions in the womb, and later by good care and education. Some object to extending these efforts to the genetic level, but, again, this is something we already do. We don't have children by no matter who and, moreover, couples who want to start a family, already hope to pass their best genetic qualities to their children. Often these expectations don't prove realistic. In cloning the genetic cards are not shuffled (apart from the mitochondrial DNA present in the egg if the cell nucleus donor is not also the egg donor). Thus cloning, in that it avoids the genetic lottery, can, if the genotype to be cloned is well selected, not only prove a way of minimising genetic risk but also an effective way for couples whose combined genes pose particular and enhanced risk of passing on genetic diseases to reproduce children genetically related to at least one of them.

13. Solipsism

It is doubtful whether people who would clone themselves would believe that it is only they who really exist; but the idea of doing it alone, unaided, without recourse or referral to others, or creating a child without the need for a sexual partner or even a gamete donor has attractions for some people. Of course there are many elements here and not all who don't want a sexual partner or gamete donor desire to 'go it alone' in other respects. Moreover, since the technology requires the co-operation and assistance of many others, the solipsistic ideal could never be realised. None-the-less, the idea of being able to reproduce without the need for a partner, a willing gamete donor or indeed without the genetic contribution of anyone else, is perhaps the ultimate in independence of a sort.

I will end by identifying some cases in which cloning might be attractive for individuals facing certain sorts of problems.

NINE CASES

(1) A couple in their forties have been trying to have a child for a number of years. All attempts, including assisted reproduction, have failed. At last IVF has given them a single healthy embryo. If they implant this embryo, the chances of it surviving are small and with it will perish their last chance to have their own child. However, if they clone the embryo say ten times they can implant two embryos and freeze eight. If they are successful first time – great! If not, they can thaw out two more embryos and try again, and so on until they achieve the child they seek. If both implanted embryos survive they will achieve identical twins.[37]

(2) A couple in which the male partner is infertile. They want a child genetically related to them both. Rather than opt for donated sperm they prefer to clone the male partner knowing that from him they will get 46 chromosomes, and that from the female partner, who supplies

the egg, there will be mitochondrial DNA. Although in this case the male genetic contribution will be much the greater, both will feel, justifiably, that they have made a genetic contribution to their child. They argue that for them, this is the only acceptable way of having children of 'their own'.

(3) A couple in which neither partner has usable gametes, although the woman could gestate. For the woman to bear the child she desires they would have to use either embryo donation or an egg cloned with the DNA of one of them. Again they argue that they want a child genetically related to one of them and that it's that or nothing. The mother in this case will have the satisfaction of knowing she has contributed not only her uterine environment but nourishment and will contribute subsequent nurture; and the father, his genes.

(4) A single woman wants a child. She prefers the idea of using all her own DNA to the idea of accepting 50% from a stranger. She does not want to be forced to accept DNA from a stranger and mother 'his child' rather than her own.

(5) A couple have only one child and have been told they are unable to have further children. Their baby is dying. They want to de-nucleate one of her cells so that they can have another child of their own.

(6) A woman has a severe inheritable genetic disease. She wants her own child and wishes to use her partner's genome combined with her own egg.

(7) An adult seems to have genetic immunity to AIDS. Researchers wish to create multiple cloned embryos to isolate the gene to see if it can be created artificially to permit a form of gene therapy for AIDS.

(8) As Michel Revel has pointed out,[38] cloning may help overcome present hazards of graft procedures. Embryonic cells could be taken from cloned embryos prior to implantation into the uterus, and cultured to form tissues of pancreatic cells to treat diabetes, or brain nerve cells . . . could be genetically engineered to treat Parkinson's or other neurodegenerative diseases.

(9) Jonathan Slack has recently pioneered headless frog embryos. This methodology could use cloned embryos to provide histocompatible[39] formed organs for transplant into the nucleus donor.[40]

We have so far considered briefly both the fears provoked by cloning and also its fascination and its possible advantages. We must now consider in more detail the substantial arguments for and against.

Two

Human reproductive cloning may be credited with one very important and successful by-product before the product itself has even a single prototype. This parasitic industry is devoted to the production of arguments against human reproductive cloning in all or any of its possible forms or applications. We have already noticed some of these products and in this chapter we will look at some appeals to very lofty and resonant ideas which are supposed either to undermine or sometimes support the moral respectability of cloning.

HUMAN DIGNITY

The idea and ideal of human dignity has been much invoked in discussions of the ethics of cloning. Typical of appeals to human dignity was that contained in the World Health Organisation statement on cloning issued on 11 March 1997.

> WHO considers the use of cloning for the replication of human individuals to be ethically unacceptable as it would violate some of the basic principles which govern medically assisted procreation. These include respect for the dignity of the human being . . .

Appeals to human dignity are of course universally attractive, they are the political equivalents of motherhood and apple pie. Like motherhood, if not apple pie, they are also comprehensively vague. A first question to ask when the idea of human dignity is invoked is: whose dignity is attacked and how? It is sometimes said, and indeed is implied in the WHO statement quoted above, that it is the duplication of a large part of the human genome, so-called 'replication', that is supposed to constitute the attack on human dignity, it being supposedly incompatible with human dignity to have someone else walking the earth in possession of 'my genes'. It is difficult to grasp the nature of the supposed problem here. Does it lie in the supposed hubris of attempting to repeat a chance or God-given combination of genes, or is it rather the issue of 'genetic identity', that somehow my uniqueness as an individual, my sense of who I am, is supposedly somehow undermined? Is it supposed to be as if I were to come home to find my look-alike with his feet under my table, planning to sleep with my wife and alienate the affections of my children? This is an unlikely scenario, the only way it could happen is if I had been cloned at birth and my clone was perpetrating this deception or usurpation.

GOD – THE GREATEST CLONING TECHNOLOGIST

But why don't we fear the real equivalent of this scenario describing a usurping clone who threatens our sense of identity and indeed our place in the scheme of things? The truth already explored is that cloning is a technology with which the human species has had a long and on the whole happy experience. Cloning has been part of human reproduction from the very beginning. God or Nature is a habitual and a serial cloner. One in every 270 births, three per thousand, are clones, or as we more usually call them, 'identical' or 'monozygotic' twins. This means that in a country the size of the UK around 200,000 identical twins are living, ostensibly no less happily than their peers. Have the heavens fallen? Does anyone complain of this massive violation of human rights and dignity? Do siblings quake at the prospect of usurpation of their role and identity, violation of their spouses and alienation of their children?

The existence and success of identical twins is a salutary reminder both of our familiarity with clones and cloning, with its success as a reproductive technology, and with the chimerical nature of the fears provoked. Even identical triplets and quadruplets are not unknown.[1] Of course they are problematic like all multiple births, difficult for the mother and fraught with dangers for the children; but not more so than multiple births that do not share a genome. Moreover we now know that IVF has increased the monozygotic twinning rate by a factor of three or more, and although there have been many moral qualms expressed about the ethics of assisted reproduction I have not so far seen moral objections to assisted reproductive technology (ART) on the grounds that it has increased the rate of identical twins from around one in 250–270 births to one in between 40 and 80 births.[2]

There are of course some contingent differences between identical twins and cloning by CNR. Identical twins usually live contemporaneous lives (although they may not do if they are twinned in vitro and one is frozen for later implantation), One identical twin does not set out to 'make' her sibling (as may sometimes be the case with CNR), although why this difference if it occurs is morally relevant is difficult to say. The ways in which normal identical twins may or may not differ from deliberately produced clones will appear as the details of cloning are systematically explored in this book. For the moment it is important to note that in so far as it is the duplication of the genome, or the likelihood of similarity in physical appearance or genetically influenced traits, that is thought significant, we are already both familiar with and accepting of these similarities in the case of identical twins and, I would suggest, so far as the empirical evidence goes it shows incontrovertibly that there is nothing wrong with these sorts of similarities or duplications.

Since 1978 around one million babies have been created through IVF worldwide[3]. This has, presumably, increased significantly the number of 'cloned' identical twins and yet this fact has seldom if ever been cited as an argument against IVF.

Throughout this book we will have occasion to remind ourselves of the occurrence of natural clones in the form of identical twins because the existence of such clones among us and the fact that they have been a frequent occurrence throughout human history is a salutary reminder that many of the worst fears about cloning are probably baseless and certainly a gross exaggeration. Equally we will often make reference to lessons that can be learned from normal sexual reproduction, not because what happens in nature is always either good or acceptable but because where things occur in nature *and* we find them acceptable for good reasons, we would require new and persuasive arguments to show why they become unacceptable if deliberately chosen. As I shall argue throughout the course of this book such arguments are almost always entirely absent. Indeed it is difficult to imagine what they would be.

The notion of human dignity is however often linked to Kantian ethics and thus apparently lent more weight and 'authority', and it is this link I wish to examine more closely now.

A typical example, and one that attempts to provide some basis for objections to cloning based on human dignity, was Axel Kahn's invocation of this principle in his commentary on cloning in *Nature*. Kahn, a distinguished molecular biologist, helped draft the French National Ethics Committee's report on cloning. In *Nature* Kahn states:[4]

> The creation of human clones solely for spare cell lines would, from a philosophical point of view, be in obvious contradiction to the principle expressed by Emmanuel Kant: that of human dignity. This principle demands that an individual – and I would extend this to read human life – should never be thought of as a means, but always also as an end.

This Kantian principle, invoked without any qualification or gloss, is seldom helpful in medical or bio-science contexts.[5] As formulated by Kahn, for example, it would surely outlaw blood transfusions. The beneficiary of blood donation seldom thinks closely about the anonymous donor and uses the blood (and its donor) exclusively as a means to her own ends. The recipient of blood donations does not usually know of or even care about the identity of the blood donor. The donor figures in the life of the recipient of blood exclusively as a means. It may be true that because the recipient of blood donation has no attitude at all to the blood donor they may not be consciously 'treating them' in any particular way. But I believe it remains true that they are using them instrumentally, consciously or not, just as I use the animals that I eat as means to my ends without thinking of them as individuals at all. Indeed that is precisely why it is 'instrumentalisation'. The blood in the bottle has after all less identity, and is less connected with the individual from whom it emanated, than the chicken 'nuggets' on the supermarket shelf. An abortion performed exclusively to save the life of the mother would also, presumably, be outlawed by this principle.

INSTRUMENTALISATION

This idea of using individuals as a means to the purposes of others is sometimes termed 'instrumentalisation' particularly in the European context. The *Opinion of the Group of Advisers on the Ethical Implications of Biotechnology to the European Commission*[6] for example, in its statement on 'Ethical aspects of cloning techniques' uses this idea repeatedly. For example, referring to reproductive human cloning (paragraph 2.6) it states: 'Considerations of instrumentalisation and eugenics render any such acts ethically unacceptable.'

Making sense of the idea of 'instumentalisation' is not easy! If someone wants to have children in order to continue their genetic line do they act instrumentally? Where, as is standard practice in IVF, spare embryos are created, are these embryos created instrumentally?

Kahn responded in the journal *Nature* to these objections.[7] He reminds us, rightly, that Kant's famous principle states: 'respect for human dignity requires that an individual is *never* used . . . *exclusively* as a means' and suggests that I have ignored the crucial use of the term 'exclusively'. I did not of course, and I'm happy with Kahn's reformulation of the principle. It is not that Kant's principle does not have powerful intuitive force, but that it is so vague and so open to selective interpretation and its scope for application is consequently so limited, that its utility as one of the 'fundamental principles of modern bioethical thought', as Kahn describes it, is virtually zero.

Kahn himself rightly points out that debates concerning the moral status of the human embryo are debates about whether embryos fall within the *scope* of Kant's or indeed any other moral principles concerning persons; so the principle itself is not illuminating in this context. Applied to the creation of individuals which are, or will become autonomous, it has limited application. True the Kantian principle rules out slavery, but so do a range of other principles based on autonomy and rights. If you are interested in the ethics of creating people then, so long as existence is in the created individual's own best interests, and the individual will have the capacity for autonomy like any other, then the motives for which the individual was created are either morally irrelevant or subordinate to other moral considerations. So that even where, for example, a child is engendered exclusively to provide 'a son and heir' (as so often in so many cultures) it is unclear how or whether Kant's principle applies. Either other motives are also attributed to the parent to square parental purposes with Kant, or the child's eventual autonomy, and its clear and substantial interest in or benefit from existence, take precedence over the comparatively trivial issue of parental motives. Either way the 'fundamental principle of modern bioethical thought' is unhelpful.

The distinguished American philosopher Hilary Putnam re-iterates the Kantian imperative employed by Axel Kahn. Putnam imagines a scenario in which cloning is widely used by ordinary people so that they can have children 'just like so-and-so'. Putnam notes, as we have done, that there is no way that this is a rational enterprise (clones will not really be like the genome donor), but he does believe 'clones will look like the person they are cloned from'. It is important to note that this may not be so for a number of reasons. Even natural monozygotic twins born within seconds of one another are often not even physically identical, to the extent that doctors and families at delivery cannot tell by looking at the twins whether they are facing monozygotic twins or twins resulting from the fertilisation of two eggs. Moreover 'twins' separated in time by scores of years, as clones are likely to be, will be almost impossible to compare with one another. Putnam then claims that 'what horrifies us about this scenario is that, in it, one's children are viewed simply as objects, as if they were commodities like a television set or a new carpet. Here what I referred to as the Kantian maxim against treating another person only as a means is clearly violated'.

Criticising Richard Lewontin,[8] Putnam suggests that Lewontin, and by implication the arguments defended here, are confused over the meaning of the Kantian principle he has invoked. Lewontin had pointed out, surely correctly, that almost all commercial relations people have with one another are basically instrumental. However, Putnam himself seems a trifle disoriented. Putnam attempts to remedy the alleged confusion with this illustration: 'Even when someone is one's employee, there is a difference between treating that someone as a mere thing and recognising their humanity. That is why there are criteria of civilised behaviour with respect to employees but not with respect to screwdrivers'.

Putnam is of course right to say that we do indeed have 'criteria of civilised behaviour' with respect to children. This is what distinguishes not only our (humankind's), attitude to children generally, but each parent's attitude to their own child in particular. However, there is no evidence for, and indeed no plausibility in, the supposition that if people choose to use a cloned genome in order to create their own children, that these children will not be loved for themselves, let alone not treated in a civilised way. We have noted that many people have children for a purpose; to continue their genes, to provide a son and heir, to create 'a sister for Bill', to provide a support in their old age, 'because I've always wanted a child to look after', because our tribe, our ethnic group is threatened with extinction etc. etc. when, if ever, is it plausible to say that they are having children *exclusively* for such purposes?

Kant's maxim provides a plausible account of what's wrong with slavery, for example, and, if another were needed, it provides one of many objections to the Nazis. Where it conspicuously fails, is to be of any help where people use, or even think of, others *partially* in instrumental terms; as happens in employment, family relations, sexual relations, and almost any human context. As I have argued, it is almost never plausible to think that people, whose motives and intentions are almost always mixed and complex, could definitively be said to be treating others 'exclusively' as a means, unless, as with the Nazis, they treated them as slaves or literally as things.

It is therefore strange that Kahn, Putnam and others invoke the Kantian principle with such dramatic assurance, or how anyone could think that it applies to the ethics of human cloning. It comes down to this: either the ethics of human cloning turn on the creation or use of human embryos, in which case as Kahn himself says 'in reality the debate is about the status of the human embryo' and Kant's principle must wait upon the outcome of that debate. Or, it is about the ethics of producing clones who will become autonomous human persons. In this latter case, the ethics of their creation are, from a Kantian perspective, not dissimilar to other forms of assisted reproduction, or, as I have suggested, to the ethics of the conduct of parents concerned exclusively with producing an heir, or preserving their genes or, as is sometimes alleged, making themselves eligible for public housing. Debates about whether these are *exclusive* intentions can never be definitively resolved and are therefore sterile and unhelpful.

Putnam supplements his use of the Kantian principle with an interesting idea, that of a 'moral image'. Putnam accepts that such images are plural and diverse and that 'people with different moral images may lead equally good moral lives'. For Putnam any moral image must incorporate the Kantian principle which he believes is itself inspired by a moral image of autonomy 'our capacity to think for ourselves in moral matters'. He then recommends an image of the family in which 'the good parent . . . looks forward to having children who will live independently of the parents not just in a physical or an economic sense, but in the sense of thinking for themselves'. This moral image has also to incorporate a 'willingness to accept diversity'. He then asks and answers a very important question:

> But why *should* we value diversity in this way? One important reason, I believe, is precisely that our moral image of a good family strongly conditions our moral image of a good society. Consider the Nazi posters showing 'good' Nazi families. Every single individual, adult or child, male or female, is blond; no one is too fat or too thin, all the males are muscular etc.! The refusal to tolerate ethnic diversity in the society is reflected in the image of the family as utterly homogenous in these ways.

Putnam continues:

> Our moral image of the family should reflect our tolerant and pluralistic values, not our narcissistic and xenophobic ones. And that means that we should welcome rather than deplore the fact that our children are not us and not designed by us, but radically Other.
>
> Am I suggesting then, that moral images of the family which depict the members of the ideal family as all alike,

either physically or spiritually, may lead to the abominations
that the eugenics movement contributed to? The answer is,
'very easily'.

And concludes:

> But perhaps one novel human right *is* suggested by the
> present discussion: the 'right' of each new-born child to be a
> complete surprise to its parents!

I am in great sympathy with much of this, indeed I have
argued along the same lines myself.[9] For example in discussing the practice of race matching in adoption I commented:

> Why do so many people firmly believe that children should be
> like their parents, particularly in terms of their general colour
> and racial characteristics? It is difficult not to view this desire,
> and attempts to implement it, as a form of 'ethnic cleansing'.
> It smacks very much of the pressure that so many societies
> and cultures have put upon their members not to 'marry out'
> or, to put it more bluntly, not to mate with somebody of
> another tribe or race . . .
>
> It is perhaps timely to press the question: why do we
> assume that the desire for a different-race child is racially
> motivated in some discreditable way, whereas the desire for a
> same-race child is not? If we are going to suspect people's
> motives, the desire for a child of the same race is surely as
> likely to be discreditable. It is after all societies which exclude
> different races that are assumed to be racist, not societies
> which welcome and celebrate diversity. Why should this not
> be true of families?[10]

The problem I have is with Putnam's interpretation of what
follows from the attractive image that he presents. First, it does

not follow from fact that if something is inconsistent with a moral image it should be banned, or controlled; nor does it follow that those who would be deviants may be punished.[11] Not only is Putnam right to say that there are many equally good moral images, there are also many equally good interpretations of the same moral image. I accept Putnam's image but, unlike Putnam, I conclude that parents should therefore have free choice in designing their children. As I have argued at length elsewhere in the context of parents using reproductive technology, it is not wrong to choose children's phenotypic traits, such as hair colour, eye colour, gender and skin colour for example:

> Some people have objected that to choose the skin colour or racial features of children (in so far as these can be chosen – which is not very far) is an illicit form of parental preference. The phrase 'designer children' is often used pejoratively to describe the children of parents who are more concerned with fashion and pleasing themselves, than with valuing children for the children's own sake. However, we should remember that choosing a same-race or same race-mix child is also designing the child that you will have. This is no less an exercise of parental preference than is the case of choosing a different race or race mix, or, for that matter, colour.
>
> The best way both to avoid totalitarianism and to escape the possibility of racial (or gender) prejudice, either individual or social, dictating what sort of children people have, is to permit free parental choice in these matters. And to do so whether that choice is exercised by choice of procreational partner or by choice of gametes or embryo, or by genetic engineering for that matter. For such choices are for the most part likely to be as diverse as are the people making them.[12]

And, of course, the reference to genetic engineering in the above passage includes the idea of cloning. As I have suggested, I accept the high value that Putnam places on a willingness to accept diversity, and on families which embody this image of diversity (few and far between as they are). I also accept the connection of such images with the sorts of society they are likely to produce. Unlike Putnam, however, I conclude from this that we should accept diversity in family foundation including the use of cloning.

I am not of course insisting that it is clear that I am right and Putnam wrong about how to interpret the value of autonomy and diversity. What I do claim however, is that the same, or at any rate similar, moral images are guiding both approaches. In such a case, tolerance of diversity seems to require that decent people be permitted to follow their own moral images in their own way, and while we may take different views about the use of cloning, neither should foreclose the others' options.

Putnam's problem is how to make his image yield the conclusions he wants on the subject of cloning and not other equally compatible conclusions of the sort that I would draw. He has two further problems. They are whether the moral image of the family is sufficient, and sufficiently determinate, to license the limitation on the autonomy of those who wish to use cloning.

Second, do not Putnam's conclusions, and the way he interprets his moral image, rather license, and indeed encourage something else? We should note that most societies accept and use images not unlike those in the Nazi posters. An 'ideal' or idealised family, in adverts for example, or in a 'sitcom', would likely display the same homogeneity. An 'ideal' or a 'typical' Jewish family for example, or an ideal or typical

African-American family. As I have suggested, we don't normally think that people founding such families are doing something wrong when they decline to marry or procreate outside their ethnic group. If we take seriously Putnam's Parthian shot, and support a 'right of each new-born child to be a *complete* surprise to its parents'[13] we should perhaps ask what would really surprise the parents of our imagined Jewish or African-American family? The answer would surely be that they would be genuinely surprised if their children turned out to be pure Aryan types straight from the Nazi posters! And the wicked pleasure that the reverse would cause, of a Nazi family giving birth to a Jewish or African (looking) child is surely justification in itself.[14] Perhaps then we should use genetic manipulation to ensure that each family, like most good societies, is ethnically and culturally diverse, and that parents are always surprised by their offspring from the moment of birth, or even before.[15]

The more serious point here is that parents will, of course, always and inevitably be surprised by their children. If they use cloning techniques for reproduction they *may* be less surprised by their children's physical appearance, but they will, for sure, be surprised by their children's dispositions, desires, traits and so on – the more so if they expected them to be identical with those of the nucleus donor.[16] Moreover, and this should not be forgotten, if they have chosen their nucleus donor wisely, they may be less surprised by one thing. They should be less unpleasantly surprised by genetic diseases and defects, for they will not only know much about the nucleus donor, but will have had opportunities to carry out genetic tests before creating the clone. A moral image that limits these unpleasant and often catastrophic surprises is one we all should have constantly before us.

AUTONOMY AGAIN

Axel Kahn produces a bizarre twist to the argument from autonomy which we should note before continuing our discussion. Kahn defines autonomy as 'the indeterminability of the individual with respect to external human will' and identifies it as one of the components of human dignity. This is of course hopeless as a definition of autonomy; those in Persistent Vegetative State (PVS) and indeed all new-borns would on such a view have to count as autonomous! However, Kahn then asserts: 'The birth of an infant by asexual reproduction would lead to a new category of people whose bodily form and genetic make-up would be exactly as decided by other humans. This would lead to the establishment of an entirely new type of relationship between the "created" and the "creator" which has obvious implications for human dignity.'

Federico Mayor has endorsed[17] a version of this argument claiming 'Cloning would remove the uniqueness that ensures no one has chosen and instrumentalised another person's identity'. Of course Mayor has got his formulation back-to-front here. It is not the uniqueness that might ensure that no one has instrumentalised another, since the uniqueness does not precede the alleged instrumentalisation. I imagine what Mayor believes is that it is the fact that we prevent instrumentalisation that might help to ensure the uniqueness.

Either way, Kahn and Mayor are, I'm afraid, wrong on both counts. As Robert Winston has noted: 'even if straight cloning techniques were used, the mother would contribute important constituents – her mitochondrial genes, intrauterine influences and subsequent nurture'.[18] These, together with the other influences would prevent exact determination of bodily form and genetic identity. For example, differences in

On Cloning

environment, age, and *anno domini* between clone and cloned would all come into play.

Lenin's embalmed body lies in its mausoleum in Moscow. Presumably a cell of this body could be de-nucleated and Lenin's genome cloned. Could such a process make Lenin immortal and allow us to create someone whose bodily form and genetic make-up, not to mention his character and individuality, would be 'exactly as decided by other human beings'? I hope the answer is obvious. Vladimir Ilyich Ulyanov was born on 10 April 1870 in the town of Simbirsk on the Volga. It is this person who became and who is known to most of us as V.I. Lenin. Even with this man's genome preserved intact we will never see Lenin again. So many of the things that made Vladimir Ilyich what he was cannot be reproduced even if his genome can. We cannot re-create pre-revolutionary Russia; we cannot simulate his environment and education; we cannot re-create his parents to bring him up and influence his development so profoundly as they undoubtedly did; we cannot make the thought of Karl Marx seem as hopeful as it must then have done; we cannot in short do anything but reproduce his genome, and that could never be nearly enough. It may be that 'manners maketh man' but genes most certainly do not.

Autonomy, as we know from monozygotic twins, is unaffected by close similarity of bodily form and matching genome. The 'indeterminability of the individual with respect to external human will' will remain unaffected by cloning. Where then are the obvious implications for human dignity?

When Kahn asks, commenting in *Nature* on some earlier arguments of mine, 'Is Harris announcing the emergence of a revisionist tendency in bioethical thinking?', the answer must be: rather I am pleading for the emergence of 'bioethical

thinking' as opposed to the empty rhetoric which invokes resonant principles with no conceivable or coherent application
to the problem at hand.

GENETIC VARIABILITY

It is often claimed that human cloning will reduce genetic
variability with catastrophic results. The UNESCO approach to
cloning for example refers to 'the preservation of the human
genome as common heritage of humanity'. Well, normal
genetic reproduction does not preserve the human genome,
rather it constantly varies it. If *preservation* were the issue, cloning on a universal scale would be the best way to achieve that
(clearly dubious) objective. Only if all existing people were
cloned would the human genome be 'preserved' intact.
Hilary Putnam concludes the written version of his amnesty
lecture[19] with the assertion that 'What I argue is that the unpredictability and diversity of our progeny (is) an intrinsic
value . . .'. We have noted in discussing Axel Kahn's views that
it is simply false that cloning could make children anything
other than unpredictable. And, as to genetic diversity, cloning
cannot be said to impact on the variability of the human
genome; it merely repeats one infinitely small part of it, a part
that is repeated at a natural rate of about 3.5 per thousand
births.[20] Those who raise threats to the human genome as a
fear in connection with human cloning owe us an explanation of how the human genome or genetic variability might
be adversely affected.

It is a truism which has become a cliché, that genotype is
not phenotype, that genes influence, but do not determine,
what traits people will have. Putnam has postulated fairly
widespread availability of cloning. But given the cost and the
foresight required (avoidance of sexual reproduction) it is

never likely to be a standard method of reproduction anymore than is IVF. At 3.5 per thousand pregnancies, natural monozygotic twinning is already quite frequent, it is surely unlikely that even on Putnam's scenario, the cloning rate would match this. Would more than one in every 270 couples or individuals for that matter want, or be able to use, cloning technology? Suppose this rate were doubled or even tripled by cloning, would anyone even notice? If the *rate* of twinning is the issue we could of course regulate access to cloning technology rather than ban it altogether.

The resolution of the European Parliament takes a different tack. Having repeated the, now mandatory, waft in the direction of fundamental human rights and human dignity, it suggests that cloning violates the principle of equality, 'as it permits a eugenic and racist selection of the human race'. Well, so does pre-natal, and pre-implantation screening, not to mention egg donation, sperm donation, surrogacy, abortion and human preference in choice of sexual partner. The fact that a technique could be abused does not constitute an argument against the technique, unless there is no prospect of preventing the abuse or wrongful use. To ban cloning on the grounds that it might be used for racist purposes is tantamount to saying that sexual intercourse should be prohibited because it permits the possibility of rape.

The second principle appealed to by the European Parliament states, that 'each individual has a right to his or her own genetic identity'. Leaving aside the inevitable contribution of mitochondrial DNA,[21] we have seen that, as in the case of natural identical twins, genetic identity is not an essential component of personal identity[22] nor is it necessary for 'individuality'. Moreover, unless genetic identity is required either for personal identity, or for individuality, it is not clear why there should be a right to such a thing. But if there is, what are we to do about the rights of identical twins?

Suppose there came into being a life-threatening (or even disabling) condition that affected pregnant women and that there was an effective treatment, the only side-effect of which was that it caused the embryo to divide, resulting in twins. Would the existence of the supposed right conjured up by the European Parliament mean that the therapy should be outlawed? Suppose that an effective vaccine for HIV was developed which had the effect of doubling the natural twinning rate; would this be a violation of fundamental human rights? Are we to foreclose the possible benefits to be derived from human cloning on so flimsy a basis? We should recall the natural occurrence of monozygotic (identical) twins. How are we to regard human rights violations on such a grand scale?

Clearly the birth of Dolly and the possibility of human equivalents has left many people feeling not a little uneasy, if not positively queasy at the prospect. It is perhaps salutary to remember that there is no necessary connection between phenomena, attitudes or actions that make us uneasy, or even those that disgust us, and those phenomena, attitudes, and actions that there are good reasons for judging unethical. Nor does it follow that those things we are confident *are* unethical must be prohibited by legislation or controlled by regulation. These are separate steps which require separate arguments.

MORAL NOSE

The idea that moral sentiments, or indeed, gut reactions, must play a crucial role in the determination of what is morally permissible is tenacious. This idea, originating with David Hume (who memorably remarked that morality is 'more

properly felt than judg'd of') has been influential in the work
of a number of contemporary moral philosophers,[23] in particular, Mary Warnock has made it a central part of her own
approach to these issues. Briefly the idea is:

> If morality is to exist at all, either privately or publicly, there
> must be some things which, regardless of consequences
> should not be done, some barriers which should not be
> passed.
>   What marks out these barriers is often a sense of outrage,
> if something is done; a feeling that to permit some practice
> would be indecent or part of the collapse of civilisation.[24]

A recent, highly sophisticated and thoroughly mischievous
example in the context of cloning comes from Leon R. Kass.
In a long discussion entitled 'The wisdom of repugnance'
Kass tries hard and thoughtfully to make plausible the thesis
that thoughtlessness is a virtue.

> We are repelled by the prospect of cloning human beings not
> because of the strangeness or novelty of the undertaking, but
> because we intuit and feel, immediately and without
> argument, the violation of things that we rightfully hold dear.[25]

The difficulty is, of course, to know when one's sense of
outrage is evidence of something morally disturbing and
when it is simply an expression of bare prejudice or something even more shameful. The English novelist George
Orwell[26] once referred to this reliance on some innate sense
of right and wrong as 'moral nose', as if one could simply
sniff a situation and detect wickedness. The problem, as I have
indicated, is that nasal reasoning is notoriously unreliable,
and olfactory moral philosophy, its theoretical 'big brother'
has done little to refine it or give it a respectable foundation.

We should remember that in the recent past, among the many discreditable uses of so-called 'moral feelings', people have been disgusted by the sight of Jews, black people and indeed women being treated as equals and mixing on terms of equality with others. In the absence of convincing arguments, we should be suspicious of accepting the conclusions of those who use nasal reasoning as the basis of their moral convictions.

In Kass's suggestion (he disarmingly admits revulsion 'is not an argument'), the give-away is in his use of the term 'rightfully'. How can we know that revulsion, however sincerely or vividly felt, is occasioned by the violation of things we rightfully hold dear unless we have a theory, or at least an argument, about which of the things we happen to hold dear we *rightfully* hold dear? The term 'rightfully' implies a judgement which confirms the respectability of the feelings. If it is simply one feeling confirming another, then we really are in the situation Wittgenstein lampooned as buying a second copy of the same newspaper to confirm the truth of what we read in the first.

We should perhaps also note for the record that cloning was not anticipated by the Deity in any of his (or her) manifestations on earth; nor in any of the extant holy books of the various religions. Ecclesiastical pronouncements on the issue cannot therefore be evidence of God's will on cloning, and must be examined on the merits of the evidence and argument that inform them, like the judgements or opinions of any other individuals.

IS IT POSSIBLE TO BE TOO REASONABLE?

One small beacon of relative sanity has been the Shapiro Report, the report commissioned by President Clinton from the National Bioethics Advisory Commission, the predecessor of President George W. Bush's President's Council.[27] Basically the Shapiro Report took the line that cloning is as yet insufficiently well-developed or understood to be regarded as safe for use in humans. Therefore because it is unsafe it would be unethical to permit an unsafe procedure to be used. Shapiro therefore recommends '[F]ederal legislation should be enacted to prohibit anyone from attempting . . . to create a child through somatic cell nuclear transfer cloning'. However, there are two important features of the Shapiro Report that are worthy of attention. The first is that it explicitly emphasises that '[I]t is critical . . . that such legislation include a sunset clause to ensure that Congress will review the issue after a specified time period (three to five years) in order to decide whether the prohibition continues to be needed.' Second, the report, almost uniquely among publicly sponsored reactions to Dolly, pays very detailed attention to the moral and policy arguments on both sides. It misses, however, one important opportunity. Having spelled out the arguments it makes no assessment of them, it merely recommends further widespread examination of the arguments in public fora. Since none of the arguments against cloning it reviews have any more plausibility than those we have just considered, there seems little to be gained by further reflection on, or indeed iteration of them. We need authoritative analysis quite as much as authoritative consideration of the arguments.

DOES THE LEGISLATIVE RESPONSE TO DOLLY CONSTITUTE AN ATTACK ON HUMAN RIGHTS AND DIGNITY?

The hysteria we have examined is of course fascinating. It tells us (we must presume) a great deal about the subconscious of the hysterics involved. It is also very disturbing because the individuals concerned occupy positions of power and influence worldwide and their gut reactions and prejudices have been translated into resolutions and regulations which are likely to prove seriously prejudicial to human welfare, and – more germane to our present concerns – to human rights.

Where nasal reasoning and olfactory moral philosophy generate bad arguments and these are deployed in the cause of limitations on human rights and freedoms, this can itself constitute a grave attack on those freedoms. Few believe, or are prepared to admit, that human rights and freedoms may be restricted on a whim, or simply to assuage feelings of unease or even of revulsion or to protect beliefs that are themselves expressions of prejudice or bigotry. One of the hallmarks of a moral position is the preparedness to deploy evidence and argument in its support. Where these are deployed they not only demonstrate the reasons for accepting the moral position and the *adequacy* of those reasons, but they also establish the position as morally respectable (if not correct) and its adherents as moral beings deserving of our respect. Where the arguments deployed in support of a moral position are inadequate or flawed then the position is left without justification and support and the conclusions which flow from it are unpersuasive. Where, however, the arguments are so thin, or implausible as to be absurd, then not only is the position in support of which they are adduced unsupported, the moral integrity of those advancing it is undermined.

This, I judge to be, is the current position with respect to arguments against human cloning. Where, as is now the case, human cloning is the object of an effective worldwide moratorium backed in some cases by international resolutions and regulations, then those resolutions and regulations are without foundation or intellectual support.

My own view, which is, for once, widely shared, is that a fundamental principle of the morality of all democratic countries is that human liberty should not be abridged without good cause being shown. Now where the liberty in question is trivial or vexatious, or is itself morally dubious or even morally neutral, it is plausible to claim that no harm is thereby done; particularly where popular support for the limitation of this supposed freedom can be demonstrated. However, where a case can be made to the effect that the freedom which has been abridged is not only not trivial, vexatious or morally dubious but rather is itself the expression of or a dimension of something morally significant, then its abridgement becomes a serious matter.

The more so when we consider some of the likely candidates for human cloning. Everyone has in mind *The Boys from Brazil* scenario of maniacs choosing to clone Hitler's genome (but not of course Hitler despite their hopes to the contrary) umpteen times in the jungles of South America. However, the fantasies of film makers or megalomaniacs should not distort our response to real concerns and genuine need. We have examined one possible (but not very likely) compelling use of human cloning. Let us now look at a number of very likely cases which might be made for human cloning and test our intuitions about them before going on to examine the hard arguments for reproductive autonomy. We will assume in all cases that human cloning by nuclear substitution is as safe as was IVF when it was first performed.

PROCREATIVE AUTONOMY AND THE RIGHT TO
FOUND A FAMILY

We have examined the arguments for and against permitting the cloning of human individuals. At the heart of these questions is the issue of whether or not people have rights to control their reproductive destiny and, so far as they can do so without violating the rights of others or threatening society, to choose their own procreative path. We have seen that it has been claimed that cloning violates principles of human dignity. We will conclude by briefly examining an approach which suggests rather that *failing* to permit cloning might violate principles of dignity.

The American philosopher and legal theorist Ronald Dworkin has outlined the arguments for a right to what he calls 'procreative autonomy' and has defined this right as 'a right to control their own role in procreation unless the state has a compelling reason for denying them that control'.[28] Arguably, freedom to clone one's own genes might also be defended as a dimension of procreative autonomy because so many people and agencies have been attracted by the idea of the special nature of genes and have linked the procreative imperative to the genetic imperative.

> The right of procreative autonomy follows from any competent interpretation of the due process clause and of the Supreme Court's past decisions applying it. . . . The First Amendment prohibits government from establishing any religion, and it guarantees all citizens free exercise of their own religion. The Fourteenth Amendment, which incorporates the First Amendment, imposes the same prohibition and same responsibility on states. These provisions also guarantee the right of procreative autonomy.[29]

The point is that the sorts of freedoms which freedom of religion guarantees, freedom to choose one's own way of life and live according to one's most deeply held beliefs are also at the heart of procreative choices. And Dworkin concludes:

> that no one may be prevented from influencing the shared
> moral environment, through his own private choices, tastes,
> opinions, and example, just because these tastes or opinions
> disgust those who have the power to shut him up or lock
> him up.[30]

Thus it may be that we should be prepared to accept both some degree of offence and some social disadvantages as a price we should be willing to pay in order to protect freedom of choice in matters of procreation and perhaps this applies to cloning as much as to more straightforward or usual procreative preferences.[31]

The nub of the argument is complex and abstract but it is worth stating at some length. I cannot improve upon Dworkin's formulation of it.

> The right of procreative autonomy has an important place . . .
> in Western political culture more generally. The most
> important feature of that culture is a belief in individual
> human dignity: that people have the moral right – and the
> moral responsibility – to confront the most fundamental
> questions about the meaning and value of their own lives for
> themselves, answering to their own consciences and
> convictions. . . . The principle of procreative autonomy, in a
> broad sense, is embedded in any genuinely democratic
> culture.[32]

The rationale that animated the principle of procreative autonomy was made the subject of a submission to the United States Court of Appeals by Ronald Dworkin and a group of other prominent philosophers. Their submission was in a case concerning voluntary euthanasia, and it is interesting because it cites a number of United States Supreme

Court decisions and their rationale. The rationale produced in these cases is relevant to us here, and below I quote at some length from *The Philosopher's Brief*:

> Certain decisions are momentous in their impact on the character of a person's life – decisions about religious faith, political and moral allegiance, marriage, procreation and death, for example. Such deeply personal decisions reflect controversial questions about how and why human life has value. In a free society, individuals must be allowed to make those decisions for themselves, out of their own faith, conscience and convictions. This Court has insisted, in a variety of contexts and circumstances, that this great freedom is among those protected by the Due Process Clause as essential to a community of 'ordered liberty'. *Palko v. Connecticut*, 302 U.S. 319, 325 (1937)

> In its recent decision in *Planned Parenthood v. Casey*, 505 U.S. 833, 851 (1992), the Court offered a paradigmatic statement of that principle:

> matters involving the most intimate and personal choices a person may make in a lifetime, choices central to a person's dignity and autonomy, are central to the liberty protected by the Fourteenth Amendment.

> As the Court explained in *West Virginia State Board of Education v. Barnette*, 319 U.S. 624, 642 (1943):

> If there is any fixed star in our constitutional constellation, it is that no official . . . can prescribe what shall be orthodox in politics, nationalism, religion, or other matters of opinion or force citizens to confess by word or act their faith therein.

In note 1.1 to *The Philosophers' Brief* it is argued that:

Interpreting the religion clauses of the First Amendment, this Court has explained that 'the victory for freedom of thought recorded in our Bill of Rights recognizes that in the domain of conscience there is a moral power higher than the State.' *Girouard v. United States*, 328 U.S. 61, 68 (1946).

And, in a number of Due Process cases, this Court has protected this conception of autonomy by carving out a sphere of personal family life that is immune from government intrusion. See e.g., *Cleveland Bd. of Educ. v. LeFleur*, 414 U.S. 632, 639 (1974) ('This Court has long recognized that freedom of personal choice in matters of marriage and family life is one of the liberties protected by the Due Process Clause of the Fourteenth Amendment.'); *Eisenstadt v. Baird*, 405 U.S. 438, 453 (1973) (recognizing right 'to be free from unwarranted governmental intrusion into matters so fundamentally affecting a person as the decision to bear and beget a child');

Skinner v. Oklahoma, 316 U.S. 535, 541 (1942) (holding unconstitutional a state statute requiring the sterilization of individuals convicted of three offenses, in large part because the state's actions unwarrantedly intruded on marriage and procreation, 'one of the basic civil rights of man');

Loving v. Virginia, 388 U.S. 1, 12 (1967) (striking down the criminal prohibition of interracial marriages as an infringement of the right to marry and holding that 'the freedom to marry has long been recognized as one of the vital personal rights essential to the orderly pursuit of happiness by free men').[33]

These decisions recognize as constitutionally immune from state intrusion that realm in which individuals make 'intimate and personal' decisions that define the very character of their lives.

In so far as decisions to reproduce in particular ways or even using particular technologies constitute decisions concerning central issues of value, then arguably the freedom to make them is guaranteed by the constitution (written or not) of any democratic society, unless the state has a compelling reason for denying them that control. To establish such a compelling reason the state (or indeed a federation or union of states, like the European Union for example) would have to show that more was at stake than the fact that a majority found the ideas disturbing or even disgusting.

Federico Mayor has attempted to deny that fundamental principles about the liberty to reproduce and to found a family are at issue in the case of cloning. Referring to the *Universal Declaration of Human Rights* Mayor says:

> Article 16 defends a basic component of human life against political prohibitions, not the 'right' to use any technology to overcome physiological impediments to natural reproduction.[34]

Of course Mayor is entitled to attempt to interpret the expression of the basic value to be found in Article 16. However, Mayor neither explains, elaborates nor defends his interpretation, he merely stipulates it. The right to found a family protected by Article 16 is at once wider, and I believe more profound, than the right to reproductive autonomy or liberty defended by Dworkin and others. This right clearly embraces the multiplicity of ways in which families might be founded, and I believe recognises that families are very diverse and do not simply include members meeting certain criteria of genetic relatedness, still less criteria that might refer to the ways in which family membership arose. Families have always been diverse. Both in the ways family relationships are established, and in the ways family ties are forged and maintained.

However, Article 16, if it is to be coherent at all, must include the right to procreative autonomy as elaborated and defended above. If this is right, a *prima facie* case has been made against Mayor's, I believe excessively, restrictive interpretation of so basic and fundamental a value.

As yet, in the case of human cloning, such compelling reasons have not been produced. True, procreative autonomy will not cover all proposed cases of human cloning (for example cases 7–9 above). Suggestions have been made, but have not been sustained, that human dignity may be compromised by the techniques of cloning. Dworkin's arguments and the cases cited in the brief above suggest that human dignity and indeed democratic constitutions may be compromised by attempts to limit procreative autonomy, at least where greater values cannot be shown to be thereby threatened. I have argued that no remotely plausible arguments exist as to how human cloning might pose significant dangers or threats or that it may compromise important human values. It has been shown that there is a *prima facie* case for regarding human cloning as a dimension of procreative autonomy that should not lightly be restricted.

JOHN ROBERTSON

John Robertson, a leading defender of procreative liberty, has interpreted this idea in a rather more restrictive form. For Robertson, otherwise a determined liberal, procreative liberty is about reproduction narrowly conceived as the reproduction of one's own genetic inheritance. He rejects as dimensions of reproduction properly so called, the reproduction of the genes of others (as in some forms of assisted reproduction or in cloning); or as the rather more extensive 'right to found a family' which would embrace founding families by adoption or other less formal methods. For Robertson, procreation 'consists of strands of varying interests in the conception and gestation of offspring'.[35] Defending his conception of the *modern traditionalist* approach to reproductive liberty in a recent paper, Robertson clearly states that someone who uses cloning to create a child with the genes of a third party (that is with the genes of someone other than the intended parent or parents) cannot claim that they are exercising reproductive liberty. 'Their claim to be exercising reproductive freedom has no basis if they are cloning a third party whom they think has a desirable genome, for in that case they would not be providing any genes and thus would not be reproducing.'[36]

Robertson here seems to be in the grip of a sort of genetic essentialism of a particularly narrow sort; one moreover which is inconsistent with important elements of his whole approach to these issues. Superficially, Robertson, like Dworkin, seems to have his 'eyes on the prize'. The prize is a broad and liberal conception of the human purposes and social institutions of which procreation is a paradigm case. Classically Robertson defends procreative liberty by reminding us that we need to consider many different concerns when assessing the scope of procreative liberty. Thus in glossing his conception of what procreative liberty embraces, Robertson asks: 'What activities related to avoiding or engaging in reproduction does a coherent conception of procreative liberty include? This can be determined only by assessing the role that those other activities play in avoiding or engaging in reproduction. Some activities seem so closely associated with or essential to reproductive decisions that they should be considered part of it, and judged by the same standards'.[37] This is close to Dowrkin's formulation quoted above: 'The right of procreative autonomy has an important place . . . in Western political culture more generally. The most important feature of that culture is a belief in individual human dignity: that people have the moral right – and the moral responsibility – to confront the most fundamental questions about the meaning and value of their own lives for themselves, answering to their own consciences and convictions. . . . The principle of procreative autonomy, in a broad sense, is embedded in any genuinely democratic culture.' Apparently for both Dworkin and Robertson these 'fundamental questions about the meaning and value of their own lives' are epitomised by the procreative endeavour, the attempt to found a family and have and rear children. For Robertson, however, this pre-occupation with having children and founding a family is only a liberty or claim-right if one's own genes are part of the deal.

There seem to me to be two powerful reasons for rejecting this sort of genetic essentialism when it comes to procreative liberty or the claim-right to found a family. The first is that the procreative enterprise seems both intentionally and culturally to have more to do with founding a family and having and rearing children than it does with the more narrow, and more recently identified, so-called 'genetic imperative'. Second it seems to say to those who have families that include children not genetically related to the parents, that they are somehow not genuine families, and that the children are not the sons and daughters of their parents and the brothers and sisters of all the other children in the family. This is gratuitously insulting to members and founders of such families and to all the adopted children and members of happy and close non-genetic or partially genetic families that have ever existed.[38]

Whatever procreation originally meant, the liberty claimed in its name has more to do with the importance and value attached to founding a family or having children than it does to a narrower sense of 'producing offspring'.[39] This is why I think the *Universal Declaration of Human Rights* better captures the core idea. But even if Robertson's narrower sense is insisted upon, Robertson cannot make it bear his excessively narrow interpretation in a way that excludes many forms of assisted reproduction. For when I want to have children, and do so by gamete or embryo donation, or by cloning a third party, I am 'producing offspring'; they are just not sprung-off my genome, but that of someone else. But I most certainly am doing the producing and the reproducing.

However, Robertson is surely right when he says: 'Like most moral and legal rights in liberal society, procreative liberty is primarily a negative claim-right – a right against interference by the state or others with reproductive decisions – not a positive right to have the state provide resources or other persons provide the gametes, conception, gestation or medical services necessary to have or not have offspring'.[40] As such and unless there are other powerful arguments against cloning, there is as strong a claim against the state not to interfere in our use of cloning as there is for any other reproductive technology. Whether or not there are any such other powerful arguments we will see in the next chapter.

Three

The interests or welfare of the child are rightly central to any discussion of the ethics of reproduction[1] and hence to the ethics of human reproductive cloning. The problematic nature of this legitimate concern is seldom, if ever, noticed, or if it is, it is misunderstood. A prominent example of this sort of misunderstanding occurs in the Department of Health's important 'Surrogacy Review' chaired by Margaret Brazier[2] (*The Brazier Report*) and the same misunderstanding makes nonsense of at least one provision of the Human Fertilization and Embryology Act 1990 (The HFE Act) which governs assisted reproduction in the United Kingdom. I will examine formulations of appeals to child welfare in these two sources because they are more fully articulated than in some of the critiques of human reproductive cloning. However, the issues are the same, they concern the coherence and legitimacy of fears that children born as a result of controversial reproductive processes or decisions may thereby suffer in unacceptable ways.

When regulation of procreation prevents some people from having children, *The Brazier Report* notes that 'there is no child who suffers this loss or to whom we or the parents have moral obligations'. The Review continues: 'Therefore, we do not have to show certainty of major harm to potential children before we are justified, either through personal decision or legislative restriction, in avoiding conceptions on grounds of risk to the welfare of the child. It is sufficient to show that, if such lives are brought into being, they could be significantly compromised physically or emotionally'.[3] *The Brazier Report* ends its discussion of child welfare with an endorsement[4] of the appropriateness of child welfare provisions such as those contained in The HFE Act.

Clause 13.5. of that Act states:

> A woman shall not be provided with treatment services unless account has been taken of the welfare of the child who may be born as a result of the treatment (including the need of that child for a father), and of any other child who may be affected by the birth.

Both these approaches, defending, or embodying, fairly comprehensive legislative interference in procreation, allegedly in the interest of the child who may be born, are fatally flawed as we shall now see.

There are very different sorts of concerns that people may legitimately have about the welfare of future children, but both the logic and the morality of the questions these concerns prompt, and the choices they represent, are crucially different. One is personal, the other more general.

THE PERSONAL QUESTION

This question concerns the interests and welfare of the child who may be born as a result of the decisions that someone will make. Here the question to be addressed is 'will the child who may result be benefited or harmed by our decision – what should we do, or permit to be done, if we care about *that child's* interests'? This question is a personal one centred on the issue of whether or not a person's reproductive choice is in the interests of the child that may result from that choice. It is this question that both The HFE Act and *The Brazier Report* ask.[5]

THE GENERAL QUESTION

The general question is concerned with what sorts of children there should be.[6] It asks what sorts of things people are better off without and therefore what things affecting people's lives we should attempt to maximise or minimise in future generations? It is not, however, concerned with the interests of any particular children but addresses the interests of children, people, in general.

The answers to neither question justify the prohibitions and regulations embodied in The HFE Act or recommended by *The Brazier Report* nor, more importantly do they support oft-repeated objections to human reproductive cloning from the perspective of the interests of the cloned child. It is important to see why.

1. PERSONAL CONSIDERATIONS

An individual's concern for, and responsibilities to, a child that may result from her decisions has many dimensions. Two principal ones, however, are what might be termed 'threshold considerations' and 'person affecting considerations'. Threshold considerations are concerned with whether or not to attempt to produce (or to continue with the attempt to produce) a person who will be affected in certain ways. Person affecting considerations come into play once the decision to bring a person into being has been taken.[7]

Threshold considerations

The personal threshold question is: 'Would I, or anyone, wrong this child by bringing it into being, or permitting it to be brought into being, in the condition and with the level of welfare that can be foreseen?' The only plausible answer to this question is one that is seldom noticed, for example by those appealing to clause 13.5 of The HFE Act. For, unless the child's condition and circumstances can be predicted to be so bad that it would not have a worthwhile life, a life worth living, then it will always be in that child's interests, to be brought to being.[8] If future children may be said to have interests at all, then it is palpably in the interests of any child, whose life will likely be worth living overall, that the threshold is crossed bringing it into being. It is, after all, that child's ('the child who may be born as a result of the treatment') only chance of existing at all.

The Brazier Report suggests that those who argue as we have just done are confused.[9] Talking of the need for regulation, it states: 'The central purpose of such regulation should be to ensure . . . that the highest priority is given to the welfare of the child to be born.'[10] But, if the welfare of that child is to have any place, we need to think about what is in fact in the interests of the child to be born as a result of assisted reproduction (AR) or surrogacy. If this were not the pertinent question we would have no reason to think of regulating surrogacy or AR in the interests of the 'child to be born'. But, unless that child would clearly not be able to lead a worthwhile life, a life that the child, and later the adult, would find acceptable; then it is clearly in the welfare and other significant interests of that child to be permitted to realise its only opportunity for existence and to be allowed to benefit from the worthwhile life that it will have. In such a case it would not be plausible to claim, as does The Brazier Report, that 'it is sufficient to show that if such lives are brought into being they could be significantly compromised physically or emotionally' for it would be emphatically in the interests of those children to exist despite the vague possibility of a life compromised to some unknown degree.

The 'child to be born' may not of course be a single individual, identifiable in advance, although contrary to widespread belief it sometimes will be; for example with pre-implantation embryos or with intra cytoplasmic sperm injection (ICSI) (where a single sperm and a single egg are identified prior to conception). However, the point holds good, 'the child who may be born . . .' is any child who may be born as a result of those acts or decisions, and it is that child's welfare that is at issue.

Person affecting considerations

We have noted that person affecting considerations come into play once the threshold decision, the decision to bring a person into being, has been taken. Once this decision has been taken then there is of course a very strong obligation not to harm the future person or seriously damage his or her welfare or other significant needs or interests. There is obviously a strong obligation not to damage a fetus in utero, for example by taking drugs that would damage its hearing or stunt its growth. The question as to whether or not it might be legitimate, knowingly to risk inflicting deafness for example, on a child not necessarily affected by that condition, is a person affecting decision.

On the other hand, the question as to whether those who have genes with significant risk of deafness should reproduce, if doing so necessarily involves passing on that condition, is a threshold question about the welfare of the 'child to be born'.

It cannot be a justification for deafening someone with normal hearing that the deaf lead worthwhile lives.

Recognising that I ought not to *worsen* my child's prospects is distinct from the question as to whether my child's prospects are so bad that I would do wrong to bring it into being.

2. GENERAL CONSIDERATIONS

The general question asks what sort of people should there be? It is interested in what, all things considered, would be best for future generations. It is not interested in the welfare of particular individuals. This general concern with the well-being of future generations addresses questions like whether or not it is better, all things considered, for children to have two parents, or not to be reared in poverty, or to be free from certain diseases or genetic conditions which might compromise him or her physically or emotionally. These general child welfare considerations would include almost anything that people feel conducive to the welfare or interests of people generally. These would of course include issues like whether or not it is better for children to be brought up believing in God, or following a particular religious faith, or in a very strict, or a very liberal environment, or facing an uncertain future.

General considerations are directed to possible futures. In relation to cloning for example a general concern would express itself by asking which of two possible children would have the better life, where one would be produced by cloning and the other not. But where the choice is not between two different possible children, but rather, as is more usual in AR or surrogacy, between having a child by these means or having no child at all, the moral question about child welfare necessarily shifts from the general to the personal.

The general question asks which sorts of children would be better? The personal question asks whether the 'child to be born' will have a life worth living despite possible sub-optimalities.

3. THE GENERAL AND THE PERSONAL IN *THE BRAZIER REPORT* AND THE HFE ACT

It is one thing to recognise that something is relevant to the welfare of children; to think, in the words of *The Brazier Report*, that 'they *could be*[11] significantly compromised physically or emotionally'. It is quite another to think that absence of such a possibly compromising feature must be *guaranteed* to children, or that it would be wrongful to permit them to come into being facing such a compromising risk (however remote). We all have views about these general welfare considerations and for some of us these will provide strong reasons to have children or not to have children. However, I think it is possible to see that there are major differences between the force of personal considerations and general considerations. The major difference is that having a view about what sort of children there should be, however rationally defensible such a view is, implies very little about the legitimacy of others producing children that do not match the ideal.

Where it is rational to judge that an individual would not have a worthwhile life if they were to be brought into being in particular circumstances, then we have not only powerful reasons not to make such choices ourselves, but also powerful moral reasons for preventing others from so doing if we can; by legislation or regulation if necessary. However, where we judge the circumstances of a future person to be less than ideal, but not so bad as to deprive that individual of a worthwhile existence, then we lack the moral justification to impose our ideals on others who would produce new children who are likely to have less than optimal lives. This is particularly true when, as is the case with AR or surrogacy, there is absolutely no empirical evidence of harms, simply a feeling that there 'could be' such harms. We should note, however, that while it is in the interests of the child who will be born with a disability to be born, unless the disability will totally blight its life, it is not in any existing individual's interests to be harmed unnecessarily. That is why it may not be wrong to go ahead and have a child knowing it will be born deaf, but not permissible to deafen a child.

These are difficult matters to generalise and an example may help. We may all agree that poverty is a very good predictor of bad outcomes for children and that ideally children should be brought up free from poverty and want. We may even think that if we ourselves were very poor, we would not want to have children, or not be justified in having them. It is quite another matter however, to say that the poor should not be permitted to have children or should be denied assistance with reproduction. Nor does it seem good policy to permit those with power to use their discretion to deny assistance with reproduction on such general grounds, for example as does clause 13.5 of The HFE Act, or to restrict availability of assistance with reproduction, as *The Brazier Report* recommends.

General considerations concern what we should aim at in reproduction, for example that children should be free from poverty and want. The personal question asks whether given the degree of poverty facing a particular child, we are justified in preventing its parents from procreating. The difference we are looking for is the difference between considerations, which would clearly blight the life of the resulting child, and considerations that merely would make existence sub-optimal in some sense.

4. PROCREATIVE AUTONOMY

Procreation is something universally acknowledged, to be not only one of the most important and worthwhile of human activities, but also one widely recognised to involve a fundamental value or right, namely the right to procreative autonomy. This right is explicitly recognised in *The Brazier Report*.[12] Ironically the report then goes on to justify, on the grounds of the 'welfare of the child', very severe limitations on this right for those who need particular forms of assistance with reproduction.

Suppose, for reasons of scarce resources, we had to ration access to AR. The state could provide access to AR for a thousand people each year. It would be a safe prediction that of the three hundred babies expected to result from the programme, those born to the richer parents would have better, less compromised, lives. It is not clear, to me at least, that this would justify restricting access to this programme to the rich.[13]

When *The Brazier Report* claims that for restrictions on procreation to be justified 'either through personal decision or legislative restriction . . . it is sufficient to show that, if such lives are brought into being, they could be significantly compromised physically or emotionally'[14] it dangerously conflates the ethics of personal decision-making and the ethics of state interference with individual liberty. It is true that when you or I think about whether or not we ought to have a child, knowing that it *could be* affected in particular ways, we are at liberty to take into account any morally relevant consideration, however remote or improbable. But when the state contemplates interference in important liberties, this is not the case. The state must show good and sufficient reason to curtail a fundamental liberty, which in the case of procreation, must amount to 'high probability of major harm to potential children'.[15] Otherwise procreative liberty is nothing but state permission. *The Brazier Report* is disingenuous when it says that 'when regulation is practicable and when it does not entail major state intrusion into the lives or bodily integrity of individuals, it may be ethically justifiable'.[16] The regulations proposed are a major intrusion; they effectively close the option of surrogacy for most potential users in the United Kingdom, denying them procreative autonomy.[17] True, such a thing may be ethically justifiable; but not on the grounds of a bare possibility of compromised welfare for those in whose alleged interests the decision is taken.

Neither voluntary surrogacy arrangements nor AR violate any rights; nor, as we have shown, do they raise any coherent concerns about child welfare. *The Brazier Report* and The HFE Act, violate, or recommend violations, not only of our shared morality, which attaches great importance to choice in matters of procreation, but of the right to found a family, a right or liberty protected by Article 16 of the *Universal Declaration of Human Rights* and by Article 12 of the *European Convention on Human Rights*. These ideas were examined in detail in the previous chapter. As *The Brazier Report* rightly suggests, and as we have already noted, rights to reproductive liberty or to found a family are neither of them 'an absolute right, especially since it can come into conflict with the rights of others. Procreation is not just a matter of individual freedom. It entails bringing about the life of another human, whose welfare and autonomy deserve the highest attention from the state'.[18] I cannot fault the reasoning of this passage, but it applies neither to voluntary surrogacy arrangements, whether commercial or not, nor to the case of assisted reproduction. In neither case does reproductive liberty, nor the right to found a family, conflict with any other rights whatsoever. To give the 'highest priority . . . to the welfare of the child to be born' is always to let that child come into existence, unless existence overall will be a burden rather than a benefit. Wherever that child's life, despite any predictable sub-optimality, will be thoroughly worth living, then it cannot be that child's interests which justify any decisions or regulations which would deny it opportunities for existence. The same will certainly be true of human reproductive cloning.

Legislation could and should aim at optimising circumstances for future generations. Rational measures to achieve this would include a better health-care system and measures to reduce poverty and deprivation. These ends are in no measure served by violating the reproductive liberty of the few who need assistance with reproduction, even where some welfare deficits are predictable for their children.

In view of the above one might have thought that child welfare arguments against human reproductive cloning would be difficult to defend. Arguments that appeal to child welfare are remarkably tenacious and ubiquitous, perhaps because the instinct to protect children is so strong among humans (and indeed other animals). We should therefore consider some of the ingenious ways in which child welfare has been revived as an argument against human reproductive cloning.

SOME NEW ARGUMENTS FROM ONORA O'NEILL

In the book of her Gifford Lectures, *Autonomy and Trust in Bioethics*,[19] Onora O'Neill produces a new twist on some old arguments concerning child protection in the context of Human Reproductive Cloning (Cloning) and in doing so rejects not only arguments defending cloning as a dimension of reproductive liberty, but also challenges those, including myself, who have cast doubt upon claims that cloning would be unacceptably bad for the resulting children. O'Neill's arguments are of importance considerably beyond their application to cloning since, if sustainable, they would apply to many forms of parenting including adoption and assisted reproductive technologies (ART).

Noting that I am on record as arguing that safe cloning, cloning that is safe from the medical and scientific perspective, would be morally acceptable, O'Neill insists that cloning is 'something for which no responsible parents would plan'. 'Would-be parents by cloning,' she suggests, 'who use reproductive tissue and genetic material from themselves or their relatives aim to bring into existence a child with *confused* and *ambiguous* family relationships. Family relationships are confused when *several individuals hold the role of one*; they are ambiguous when *one individual holds the roles of several*'.[20] For O'Neill, such confusion and ambiguity are anathema.

We will examine both these ideas in turn starting with confusion, something to which philosophers are instinctively opposed.

CONFUSED RELATIONSHIPS

'Where children acquire confused relationships, whether by fostering, adoption or parental remarriage, we usually see the situation as regrettable, even if unavoidable, and seek to provide them with extra legal and social protection. Confused relationships created by cloning are not less likely to burden children: Would responsible parents seek confused relationships for their children from the start?'[21]

It is not clear what O'Neill is claiming here, but her use of the idea of 'responsible parents' in the context of adoption and fostering loads the dice in a subtle way. Adoptive and foster parents must in the United Kingdom, and in many other societies, be 'screened' by adoption agencies and social services departments. Such screening is designed to identify those who would not make 'responsible parents' and disqualify them from being candidates for these forms of parenting.[22] The implication is clearly that those who would use cloning would already have disqualified themselves as would-be parents by the very fact of selecting this technology. Moreover O'Neill is somewhat tendentiously implying that it is the danger of confusion that makes the necessity of adoption and fostering regrettable and indeed makes appropriate the extra legal and social protection accorded to adoptive and foster children. I doubt the idea of confused roles figures prominently in the thoughts of any but a tiny minority of those who consider adoption or fostering a regrettable necessity, and the extra legal and social protection which most societies establish in these cases is not conspicuously targeted upon the children's clarity of mind about their relationships.[23]

Two questions immediately arise – is anyone actually confused, and how bad is confusion – is it so bad to confuse a child that no one should be permitted to do so?[24]

Of course finding themselves in circumstances in which 'several individuals hold the role of one' may confuse children; but how confused are they, how bad is the confusion and is it impossible to un-confuse them?[25] These must remain rhetorical questions as far as cloning goes, but the evidence from adoption and fostering as well as from assisted reproduction is not powerfully supportive of the idea that such dangers and disadvantages as exist in all these areas are much aggravated by multiplication of roles.[26] Indeed, when children are adopted as babies and when they result from ART (the cases closest to cloning) they are not usually confronted with any duplication of roles among their parents. They are cared for and parented by their real parents – those who do the parenting, their genetic parents, where these are not the real parents of the child in question are seldom (probably never) present, playing a confusing parental role. Many people are raised in a culture where most female adults who were frequent visitors to the house were called 'Aunty' but I have not seen compelling evidence that they have suffered overmuch from such confusion of roles.

Of course when children become of an age to understand that they have been adopted, or were produced from gametes or genes other that those of one or both of their parents they will have some interesting complexity to digest. If they are then told about their origins,[27] they may have to understand that they have both genetic and real parents, but again at this stage it is unlikely that there will be any duplication of, let alone confusion in, roles. Finally they may trace and meet their genetic parents if they so choose. Then, and almost certainly only then, they may allow both sets of parents to play parental roles, but again, they are hardly likely to be confused by this. Indeed, all the evidence is that they are well up to the task.[28]

There are of course many scenarios in which adoptive and foster children (although probably not children resulting from ART) grow up with multiple parents playing active roles at various times. Again the question of how bad this is for the children is one to which there are no solidly consistent answers, although again evidence of substantial harm is entirely missing. However, likely scenarios for reproductive cloning are unlikely to involve such multiple parenting, since those who commission the cloning process are likely to want the parenting role themselves. There may of course be a number of people who are in some sense of the term, 'parents' of the cloned children, depending on which cloning process is used and who may have a legitimate claim to the title 'parent'. We should note for the record that a woman could in theory clone herself using her own egg as the host for the nucleus of a cell from another part of her body, thus ending up as the truly identical twin sister of her cloned baby.[29] Her own parents will be the genetic parents, but unless they are also active in rearing and caring there will again be no necessary confusion of roles.

In many families older children often play the role of mother or father to their younger siblings when the parents are absent. This is certainly a confusion in O'Neill's sense ('several individuals hold the role of one') but I have not seen much in the literature about the damaging effects of this practice, nor criticisms of the irresponsibility of parents who permit it.

Equally, I seem to recall the phrase 'in loco parentis', admittedly not always from settings within the nuclear family. However when aunts and uncles, older siblings and even those not genetically related to children act 'in loco parentis' in cases of need this is seldom accompanied by charges of improper conduct or irresponsibility (at least not simply in virtue of the duplication of parental roles).

AMBIGUOUS RELATIONSHIPS

'*Ambiguous* family relationships are less common' says O'Neill, 'although they can arise by marriage between close relatives and by incest as well as by cloning. In such cases grandfather may be father, aunt may be sister. Cloning from a would-be parent is likely to produce more ambiguities even than incest within the nuclear family. Again responsible parents would not aspire for a child to have ambiguous relationships. Still less would any responsible parent plan for a child to have family relationships that are *confused* and *ambiguous*.'[30]

We should note that although O'Neill firmly distinguishes *confusion*: 'several individuals hold the role of one', and *ambiguity*: 'one individual holds the roles of several', they are often combined; since when more than one person is 'mother' one of those individuals would often also be 'grandma' or 'aunt'.

Ambiguity is a little more difficult to grasp than confusion,[31] perhaps because of the ambiguity involved; but again I find it difficult to understand just what is wrong, morally wrong, or damaging about ambiguity in relationships; unless it is through guilt by association with incest.

A single parent will often try to be both mother and father to her child, combining behaviour and activities she thinks of as distinctive of both parental roles or both dimensions of parenting. While single parenting has its problems, I for one am far from convinced that being a single parent is something 'for which no responsible parents would plan'. Many responsible parents do plan for just this outcome and the outcomes are far from worrying.[32]

O'Neill is right that when would-be parents clone one of themselves they would create a child that they intend to parent, but which would be the twin sibling of the cell nucleus donor and the genetic child of the parents of the cell nucleus donor.[33] Whether there would be any ambiguity of roles would be contingent upon the degree of participation of the parents of the cell nucleus donor in the life of that particular family. If they did 'participate' actively, it is surely unlikely that they would try to pass themselves off to the child as rival parents and thus create ambiguous roles in a psychologically problematic way.[34] True there would be ambiguity in relationships in the sense that there would be a number of family members who would be 'parents' in different senses – genetic, social and so on. However, O'Neill is herself trading on an ambiguity in the meaning of the term 'family relationship' when she says would-be cloners 'aim to bring into existence a child with *confused* and *ambiguous* family relationships'.

The ambiguity rather consists in our understanding the term 'relationship' to cover both formal relationships (whether genetic or social) 'mother', 'cousin' and so on, and the ways in which family members relate to one another – play the role of 'mother', 'cousin' etc. in the life of the child. I have seen no evidence that the mere existence of more than, let us say, one man and one woman who can lay some formal claim to the title 'parent' of a particular child causes, or has caused, the sort of damage that would justify the charge of 'irresponsible parenting'. Whether certain more active role-playing would cause problems is an interesting question to which I doubt we have any answers – it being notoriously difficult in this sort of family research to isolate causative factors.

I fear that O'Neill has elevated her distaste for cloning into a theory, or at least a position, concerning the problematic nature of confusion and ambiguity in family life. Most human relationships, including those in families, are replete with both confusion and ambiguity some of which certainly cause anxiety and unhappiness – 'does she love me?' 'Have I behaved badly?' 'Is it me or my sister who has caused this upset?' These are often necessary and productive ambiguities and confusions. We simply don't know whether the ambiguities and confusions that upset O'Neill would be more or less damaging than these.

SUB-OPTIMAL PARENTING

It is perhaps unfair to tax O'Neill too much over her selection of the notions of confusion and ambiguity as bearers of the weight of objections to cloning. She is after all making the point that where outcomes for children are predictably problematic or sub-optimal in some way, then it is fair and reasonable to ask whether responsible parents would seek to produce children in such circumstances. As I have indicated, there is little reason to believe that being a clone is necessarily problematic; but, suppose that there is some reason for apprehension. Does not a precautionary approach require that we do not expose children even to small sub-optimalities or even to small risks of being brought to being in conditions that may be bad for the child? We have, in a previous chapter, addressed the weaknesses of the precautionary principle[35] and for the sake of the argument I will assume precaution is indicated. What does this require exactly? Parents very frequently have children in circumstances which are less than ideal, and often in circumstances which might improve over time. Is this always wrong? Is this something no responsible parents would seek to do? Should a couple in their early twenties or late teens always wait for greater financial security in their late twenties or early thirties?

Poverty is the best and most consistent predictor of bad outcomes for children. Would responsible poor people have children – should the poor reproduce, should they be permitted to reproduce? These are importantly different questions. O'Neill never directly addresses the issue of compulsion or prohibition, but the implication of her approach and her tone seems strongly suggestive of the idea that we have good reason to prevent irresponsible parenting. Since poverty is something the bad effects of which are known (and which are decidedly not merely speculative) there would seem to be stronger arguments to outlaw procreation among the poor than there are to prevent cloning at least so far as O'Neill's arguments against cloning go. Moreover, given that the poor are numerous and that the numbers of people able to access cloning technology would for the foreseeable future be severely limited, the magnitude of the good done by preventing the poor from reproducing would be much the greater.

The only thing poverty seems to have going for it is that it is an existing or customary dimension of sub-optimal parenting. It is sometimes argued that there is an important difference between declining to remedy existing harms and declining to add new ones. Thus it is sometimes said that while we cannot prevent irresponsible people from parenting, using sexual reproduction as their chosen method, we can and should prevent such people accessing adoption or ART. This seems a poor argument. If it is wrong to create a new harm, it must be equally wrong to fail to prevent or remedy an existing harm of the same magnitude.[36] The wrong is doing harm or permitting harm to be done. This moral imperative must, both logically and practically, apply as much to existing as to future harms. Indeed some people (though not me) think it applies more strongly to existing harms. It certainly applies more strongly to more probable harms.[37]

I suggest however that despite sub-optimalities, we do not believe that the poor should be prevented from or even strongly discouraged from reproducing. This is partly because we accept the importance of procreative liberty,[38] we do not like the idea of the state interfering in the procreative choices of citizens, and partly because with certain quite wide limits, we believe that kids should take their chances with parents, just as we believe that parents should accept what comes when it comes to kids. This is of course not to say that parents should not attempt to choose traits for their children if these are either advantageous or neutral, rather that having done their best to make their children healthy and happy they should accept what comes.[39]

If we think that the moral importance of the procreative liberty of the poor outweighs the sub-optimalities for children which attend poverty and therefore permits their use of sexual procreation as a means of reproduction we need some additional arguments to deny others the use of cloning as a method of reproduction when the results are almost certainly less problematic and the probability of problems at present unknown.

We do however know that in the case of cloning, and usually also in the case of ART, unless these technologies are used the particular child in question will never exist.[40] A rational would-be[41] child of cloning or ART would regard the slight risk of confusion as a price well worth paying for existence, unless of course such confusion made life very terrible indeed. This is of course also sometimes true of poverty and other harms which might abate over time. If poor parents wait for better times the children they will have will be different. This is the famous non-identity problem identified by Derek Parfit.[42]

THE NON-IDENTITY PROBLEM

In this section I draw on some arguments I developed jointly with Justine Burley.[43] Consider the following two cases. The first was developed by Derek Parfit and involves a 14-year-old prospective mother.

> This girl chooses to have a child. Because she is so young, she gives her child a bad start in life. Though this will have

bad effects throughout the child's life, his life will, predictably, be worth living. If this girl had waited for several years, she would have had a different child, to whom she would have given a better start in life.[44]

An analogue to this case is:

A woman chooses to have a child through cloning. Because she chooses to conceive in this way, she gives the child a bad start in life. Though this will have bad effects throughout the child's life, his life will, predictably, be worth living. If this woman had chosen to procreate by alternative means, she would have had a different child, to whom she would have given a better start in life.

In both cases, two courses of action are open to the prospective mother. In criticising these women's pursuit of the first option available (i.e. conception at 14 and reproductive cloning respectively) people might claim that each mother's decisions will probably be worse for her child.[45] However, as Parfit notes, while people can make this claim about the decisions taken it does not *explain* what they believe is objectionable about them. It fails to explain this because neither decision can be worse for the particular children born; *the alternative for both of them was never to have existed at all*. If the 14-year-old waits to conceive, a completely different child will be born. Likewise, if the woman chooses not to clone and instead conceives by natural procreative means the child born will be a different one. Thus claims about the badness of pursuing the first option in both of the above cases cannot be claims about why *these* children have been harmed. It is better for *these* children that they live than not live at all.

This does not of course mean that parents do not have moral reasons to have different children in better

circumstances; rather it means that the reasons for not procreating, or not permitting procreation, are not that such a
course is in the interests of 'the child who may be born'.[46]
The moral reason for preferring to have children in better
rather than worse circumstances where this means that the
children will be different are because the outcome is better
overall. Or, as I would prefer to say, the world that would be
created by the decision is better than the alternative world.

INSTRUMENTALISATION AND CHILD WELFARE

In the previous chapter we looked in some detail at the notion
of instrumentalisation. I venture that, worldwide, the majority of children are conceived with nothing else in mind
but the sexual pleasure of one or both parents; the thought
(or indeed fear) of conception being far from their minds.
Thereafter absence of safe or legal abortion often ensures that
the primary motive remains effectively the only motive. Other
primary goals include 'having a son', 'continuing the genetic
line', or providing 'an heir to the family fortune'.

A FAIRYTALE

Fairytales can be very instructive, as every parent knows. So
let's consider a very well known story.

There was a prince who fell in love. But his choice lay with
someone who was, unfortunately, not a princess and was
anyway married to someone else. She was therefore considered
very unsuitable as a prospective wife. The Queen would never
let him marry a divorced 'commoner'. But it was his duty to
marry and have children to be heirs to the throne that he was
heir to. So he found a very young and beautiful princess who
didn't know any better, and married her in order to fulfil his
duty to provide heirs and become a suitable candidate to be

king when his mother died. They had two fine sons, whom of course his wife and he both loved dearly. But alas, as all the world knows, they did not live happily ever after.

Few have suggested that the fairytale prince's motives were so bad that his marriage should have been prevented or annulled, or that, failing timely state intervention, his children have been unacceptably damaged by their knowledge of their primary function as heirs to a famous throne. He may not be the best or most moral prince in the world of the imagination, but he is not accounted irredeemably wicked. In some future fairy tale he may even become king. Although many arguments have been adduced against the institution of the monarchy denial of an open future to royal children has seldom been prominent among them. Having ideals about the appropriate frame of mind for, and purposes of, procreation is a long way from evidence that those with other ideas are so immoral that legislation should prevent their procreative choices. We should not confuse our ideals and preferences for moral principles; nor should we imagine that we are entitled necessarily to enforce our preferences however strongly we hold them.

THE RIGHT TO AN OPEN FUTURE

Joel Feinberg has elaborated what he calls 'the right to an open future' in the context of child protection.[47] Such a right is a right held 'in trust' for a child to exercise when he or she has the competence that makes the right relevant. It is important to consider this argument because it often seems as though if there is a right to an open future this might preclude cloning since by hypothesis cloned children would have closed futures. Let's see how this might or might not be true. This is how Feinberg explains the right:

When sophisticated autonomy rights are attributed to
children who are clearly not yet capable of exercising them,
their names refer to rights that are to be *saved* for the child
until he is an adult, but which can be violated 'in advance' so
to speak, before the child is even in a position to exercise
them. The violating conduct guarantees *now* that when the
child is an autonomous adult, certain key options will already
be closed to him. His right while he is still a child is to have
these future options kept open until he is a fully formed, self-
determining adult capable of deciding among them.

And Feinberg concludes that all rights-in-trust of this sort
'can be summed up as the single "right to an open future" '.
Later in his essay Feinberg cites with approval a seminal court
ruling which outlines the relevant principle encapsulating the
right to an open future confirming in Feinberg's words that
children must be 'permitted to reach maturity with as many
open options, opportunities, and advantages as possible'.[48]
The judgement comes from the 1944 case of *Prince v.
Massachusetts* in the United States Supreme Court.[49]

The healthy, well rounded growth of young people into full
maturity as citizens with all that implies [in a democracy] . . .
Parents may be free to become martyrs themselves. But it
does not follow that they are free in identical circumstances
to make martyrs of their children before they have reached
the age of full and legal discretion when they can make that
decision for themselves.[50]

This case involved the children of Jehovah's Witnesses who
distributed religious tracts on the streets, and while Feinberg
notes that the principle was probably misapplied in this case
he clearly endorses its substance. Clearly Feinberg was not

addressing himself to the issue of cloning, but it is far from clear that cloning would deny cloned children an open future.

HIGH EXPECTATIONS AND NO 'OPEN FUTURE'[51]

Some people think that human clones will have psychological difficulties because people will have special expectations of them. The clone's life will always be compared to that of his or her genetic parent. It has been said that the clone will have a 'life in the shadow' of the person from whose genes he or she was cloned.[52] A clone would have the feeling that his life already had been lived and, consequently, will be deprived of 'an open future'. We know how his genetic parent lived, so we will know how the child will live. He will be considered as 'the copy' that has less quality than its original and that has no life of his own. Leon Kass, President of the United States' President's Council on Bioethics, expressed it this way: 'The cloned individual, moreover, will be saddled with a genotype that has already lived. [. . .] People are likely always to compare his performances in life with that of his alter ego. Still, one must also expect parental and other efforts to shape this new life after the original – or at least to view the child with the original version always firmly in mind. Why else did they clone from the star basketball player, mathematician, and beauty queen – or even dear old dad – in the first place?'[53]

This polemic assumes, without any evidence or plausible argument, necessarily bad motives on the part of the intentional parents who want to make use of the cloning technique to have a child. The second problem in saying that a child will not have an open future is saying that a clone will not be unique and will not develop a personal identity. The third problem with the argument is that all the concerns expressed in it are based on the assumption that people, despite all the explanations and information, will persist in their belief in genetic determinism. Since we cannot be sure that this will be the case, the argument has a hypothetical character and carries less weight. Finally, such expectations are also true of all parenting. What parent does not look at their child with themselves in mind as a model of expectation, if only a model of minimal expectation? 'I want my child to be better than me'! We saw from our fairytale that even in a radical context of parental expectation it is unlikely that burdens on children will be so great as to render unacceptable the whole practice.

SOCIETAL PREJUDICE AND RESPECT FOR CLONES

Another objection often advanced against human cloning is that the clones will be the victims of discrimination in society and will not be respected as full persons. The former chairman of the United Kingdom Human Fertilisation and Embryology Authority (HFEA), Ruth Deech, asked: 'Would cloned children be the butt of jibes and/or be discriminated against? Would they become a subcaste who would have to keep to each other? Would they be exploited? Would they become media objects?'[54]

We should note again that persons conceived through cloning will be persons like everyone else. The only difference to other people is the way in which they were conceived, namely with one somatic cell and an enucleated egg, and not with two gametes. We should not discriminate against people on the basis of the way in which they were conceived, just as we should not discriminate against people on the basis of gender, skin colour, sexual orientation, etc. It is important to note that in this objection, the source of the harm done to the future clone is not the intention of parents to have a child through cloning, but the fearful and/or prejudicial attitudes of other people towards clones. Can the fear of those discriminatory reactions be a sound ground to ban cloning? Suppose sexual orientation is genetic, and can be discovered by a simple test. Should we forbid a woman to implant an embryo which she knows as a result of pre-implantation genetic diagnosis (PGD) will result in a homosexual child and oblige her to conceive a new one in the hope that it does not have that disposition, because in our society homosexuals are discriminated against? Rather we should combat prejudices and mistaken ideas concerning homosexuals. The same is true for cloning. Moreover, a view that defends reproductive freedom and autonomy and combats prejudices and discrimination in society is more compatible with human dignity than a view which indirectly stimulates or maintains those mistaken ideas and reduces our reproductive autonomy.

Safety and Danger
Four

1. SAFETY

In previous chapters we have examined cloning from the perspective of human rights and dignity and have looked at the
extent to which the idea of procreative liberty can inform
reproductive choices, which might use cloning. We then
examined the weight, which should be given to concern for
the welfare of children that might be born as a result of cloning
technology. In this chapter we look at a plethora of disparate
arguments that, born of a desperation to find something (one
may reasonably think desperation to find *almost anything*) that
can be said against cloning, have entered the public debate.
They are a testament to the perseverance and ingenuity, which
can be deployed in defence of antipathy to cloning. At the end
of this chapter we will look again at the one remotely plausible
argument that has been levelled against human reproductive
cloning, the idea that because it is untested and possibly
unsafe, it should not for the moment be permitted.

The preservation of the human genome

'The preservation of the human genome as common heritage
of humanity' is regarded by UNESCO[1] as important and this
alleged necessity is used as an argument against cloning. What
precisely does this mean and how might cloning pose a
threat?

On Cloning

Does this mean that the human genome must be 'preserved intact', that is without variation, or does it mean simply that it must not be 'reproduced a-sexually'? Cloning cannot be said to impact on the variability of the human genome; cloning simply repeats an existing genome, but this does not reduce variability, it just does not increase it. Even if everyone in the world used cloning as his or her sole method of reproduction this would not reduce the variety of the human genome, it would simply leave the variety exactly as it was. However, because of the costs and the technical difficulty, not to mention the fact that sexual reproduction usually offers other incentives to those who use it, it is unlikely that cloning rates will ever be so high as to threaten the human gene pool or its variability.

We must change to survive?

The renewal of the gene pool is sometimes cited as a consideration which should lead to the rejection of cloning. Unless, so it is claimed, the human gene pool constantly changes through the random effects of sexual procreation, viruses and other diseases will become effective against a particular set of genotypes with disastrous consequences. There is some merit in the idea that unless there is change, a particular genotype will become increasingly vulnerable to mutating viruses or other infections of one sort or another and might not be able to change quickly enough to prevent a disaster which might wipe out our species as a whole. Of course, if everyone were to reproduce only and forever via cloning this might well be a danger, but this is so unlikely for reasons of cost, circumspection (or lack of it) and the attractions of alternative methods, that there is no real danger here.

A right to parents

It is sometimes claimed that children have 'a right to have two parents' or 'the right to be the product of the mixture of the genes of two individuals'. We mentioned this possibility in the Introduction to this book, but it is as well to remind ourselves here of this common error in considering the origin of clones. If the right to have two parents is understood to be the right to have two social parents, then it is of course only violated by cloning if the family identified as the one to rear the resulting child is a one-parent family. This is not of course necessarily any more likely a result of cloning, than of the use of any of the other new reproductive technologies (or indeed of sexual reproduction). Moreover if there is such a right, it is widely violated, creating countless 'victims', and there is no significant evidence of any enduring harm from the violation of this supposed right. Indeed the tragic existence of so many war widows throughout the world and the success most of them have in rearing their children is eloquent testimony to the exaggerated fears expressed concerning cloning.

If, on the other hand, we interpret a right to two parents as the right to be the product of the mixture of the genes of two individuals, then the supposition that this right is violated when the nucleus of the cell of one individual is inserted into the de-nucleated egg of another, is false in the way this claim is usually understood. There is at least one sense in which a right expressed in this form might be violated by cloning, but not in any way which has force as an objection. First, it is false to think that the clone is the genetic child of the nucleus donor. It is not. The clone is the twin brother or sister of the nucleus donor and the genetic offspring of the nucleus donor's own parents. Thus this type of cloned individual is, and always must be, the genetic child of two separate geno-types, of two genetically different individuals, however often it is cloned or re-cloned.

What good is cloning?

Reproductive cloning may help some people to have children genetically related to them who otherwise could not. This aside, the purely reproductive purposes of cloning are not obviously important or urgent; but that is not to say that it is a matter of indifference if cloning is banned. As I have suggested earlier, we should be reluctant to accept restrictions on human liberty however trivial the purposes without good and sufficient cause being shown.

One major reason for developing cloning in animals may be to permit the study of genetic diseases and indeed genetic development more generally. Whether or not there would be major advantages in human cloning by nuclear substitution is not yet clear. It would enable some infertile people to have children genetically related to them, it offers prospect, as we have noted, of preventing some diseases caused by mitochondrial DNA, and could help 'carriers' of X-linked and auto-somal recessive disorders to have their own genetic children without risk of passing on the disease. It is also possible that so-called therapeutic cloning could be used for the creation of 'spare parts' by, for example, growing stem cells for particular cell types from non-diseased parts of an adult or by cloning stem cells for regenerative therapies and possibly for life-extending therapies.[2]

Dolly collapses the divide between germ and somatic cells

There are some interesting implications of cloning by nuclear substitution (which have been clear since frogs were cloned by this method in the 1960s), which have not apparently been noticed.[3] There is currently a worldwide moratorium on manipulation of the human germ line, while therapeutic somatic line interventions are, in principle, permitted. Germ line interventions affect the games or 'germ cells' and are passed on indefinitely to future generations whereas interventions on the somatic line affect only the individual themselves. However, inserting the mature nucleus of an adult cell into a de-nucleated egg turns the cells thus formed into germ line cells. This has three important effects. First, it effectively eradicates the firm divide between germ line and somatic line nuclei because each adult cell nucleus is in principle 'translatable' into a germ line cell nucleus by transferring its nucleus and creating a clone. Second, it permits somatic line modifications to human cells to become germ line modifications. Suppose you permanently insert a normal copy of the adenosine deaminase gene into the bone marrow cells of an individual suffering from Severe Combined Immuno-Deficiency (which affects the so called 'bubble boy' who has to live in a protective bubble of clean air) with obvious beneficial therapeutic effects. This is a somatic line modification. If you then cloned a permanently genetically modified bone marrow cell from this individual, the modified genome would be passed to the clone and become part of his or her genome, transmissible to her offspring indefinitely through the germ line. Thus a benefit that would have perished with the original recipient and not been passed on for the protection of her children, can be conferred on subsequent generations by cloning.[4] The third effect is that it shows the oft-asserted moral divide between germ line and somatic line therapy to be even more ludicrous than was previously supposed.

Of course some individuals might wish to have offspring, not simply with their genes, but with a matching genotype. However, there is no way that they could make such an individual a duplicate of themselves. So many years later the environmental influences would be radically different, and since every choice, however insignificant, causes a life-path to branch with unpredictable consequences, the holy grail of using cloning to achieve immortality would be doomed to remain a fruitless quest. We can conclude that people who would clone themselves might be foolish and ill-advised, but it is doubtful that they would be immoral nor would their attempts harm society or their children significantly.

Therapeutic cloning coupled with stem cell research might enable the human body to repair itself indefinitely leading eventually to a kind of immortality. Some people fear this; I for one believe the dangers have been exaggerated, but since this, at the moment remote, possibility does not involve reproductive cloning I will not explore it further here.[5]

Jeremy Rifkin's arguments

Jeremy Rifkin has produced two oblique arguments against cloning which merit some attention. The first is part of his general preference for one kind of biotechnology rather than another; and the second concerns the intrusion of intellectual property issues in general, and patenting in particular into the cloning debate.

Curing disease versus preventive health

In his book *The Biotech Century*[6] Rifkin repeats his oft asserted distinction between using biotechnology 'to "correct" disorders and arrest the progress of disease', between 'efforts designed to cure people who have become ill' on the one hand, and the task of 'exploring the relationship between genetic mutations and environmental triggers with the hope of fashioning a more sophisticated, scientifically based understanding and approach to preventive health' on the other.[7] Rifkin concludes that it is wrong to pursue both methods, and judges, rightly, that the question we need to answer in order to be able to know which is preferable is: 'on balance, does it do more harm than good?'[8] Rifkin thinks he knows the answer to this one, and he sets it out as follows:

> 'First do no harm' is a well-established and long revered principle of medicine. The fact is, the more powerful a technology is at altering and transforming the natural world – that is, marshaling [*sic*] the environment for immediate, efficient and short term ends – the more likely it is to disrupt and undermine long-standing networks of relationships and create disequilibrium somewhere else in the surrounding milieu. Which of the two competing visions of biotechnology – genetic engineering or ecological practices and preventive health – is more radical and adventurous and most likely to cause disequilibrium and which is the more conservative approach and least likely to cause unanticipated harm down the line? The answer, I believe, is obvious.[9]

A number of points need to be made here. The first is that I have no objections to Rifkin's preferred use of biotechnology; but I believe there are strong grounds for resisting any attempts to make it the only approach. We need both approaches not just one; why? First, because when Rifkin asks: 'Which of the two competing visions of biotechnology . . . is . . . least likely to cause unanticipated harm down the line?' he is begging a crucial question. Although he does not produce (and indeed could not produce) any evidence for this claim, it is difficult not to see this claim as highly suspect because it implies that it is only 'down the line' harm that we have to worry about. Recall that the genetic engineering of which he disapproves is directed towards 'efforts designed to cure people who have become ill'. If such genetic engineering methods are not pursued there is a grave danger that those who have already become ill will be neglected and will suffer and perhaps die as a result. These are real and present dangers, faced by real and present people who will suffer and die if their diseases are not treated and, if research, which might help them, is not pursued. Rifkin's preferred strategy of 'ecological practices and preventive health' is directed towards preventing people becoming ill in the future, not helping those who have already become ill. We do not know which strategy will save more people overall, but we should not choose between them because that will condemn either present people to suffer and die when they might be helped or, because it will fail to make ecological changes that might prevent future disease. It is obvious that we must do both, not least because the rule of rescue requires that we do not abandon those in present need. It is normal good practice to meet real and present dangers before future and speculative ones; this idea is part of the so-called rule of rescue.

Second, we should notice that Rifkin makes another rather obviously suspect claim. He says: 'The fact is, the more powerful a technology is at altering and transforming the natural world – that is, marshaling [sic] the environment for immediate, efficient and short term ends – the more likely it is to disrupt and undermine long-standing networks of relationships and create disequilibrium somewhere else in the surrounding milieu.' Rifkin calls this a 'fact', but it is simply a piece of speculation; moreover even if it were coherent and/or true, we would need to know whether the resulting 'disequilibrium in the surrounding milieu'[10] caused harm that would not be compensated for by the good done by the powerful technology. Without these two crucial pieces of information we cannot hope to make a rational choice and all that is left to us is the pursuit of prejudice.[11]

Intellectual property

In a newspaper article[12] in 2000, Rifkin made some radical, and, as I shall demonstrate, radically misleading, claims about intellectual property issues in the context of cloning. Here is what he says:

> The British patent office has just granted Wilmut's Roslin Institute patents on his cloning process and all animals cloned using the process. The patents have been licensed to Geron Corp., a California-based biotech company. There is something more, however. The patent also includes as intellectual property – i.e., patented inventions – all cloned human embryos up to the blastocyst stage, which is a cluster of about 140 cells. For the first time, a national government has declared that a specific human being created through the process of cloning is, at its earliest phase of development, to be considered an invention in the eyes of the patent office. The implications are profound and far-reaching.
>
> It was less than 135 years ago that the United States abolished slavery, making it illegal for any human being to own another human being as property after birth. Now the British patent office has opened the door to a new era in which a developing human being can be owned, in the form of

intellectual property, in the gestational stages between conception and birth.

Regardless of where people may stand on the question of abortion, one would think that everyone would be shocked at the idea that a company might be able to own a human embryo as an invention.

Parents, when they read about this extraordinary patent decision, should ask themselves whether their children and future generations will be well served ethically if they grow up in a world where they come to think of embryonic human life as intellectual property, controlled by life science companies. What happens to our children's most basic notions about the distinctions between human life and inanimate objects when the former comes to be regarded by law as mere inventions, simple utilities to be bartered like so many commodities in the commercial arena?

And, if cloned human embryos are, in fact, considered to be human inventions, then what becomes of our notion of God, the creator? What will future generations say when their children ask, where do babies come from? Will they say they are the inventions of scientists and the property of life science companies?[13]

This is a fascinating article for a number of reasons. The first is that even if a patent of the sort Rifkin describes had been granted,[14] it would imply neither slavery nor the possibility of physical ownership of a human individual. Had such a patent been granted it would not have withstood challenge in the courts for precisely the reasons Rifkin gives, namely its incompatibility with even basic notions of human rights and with normal notions of public morals and so on. Moreover the operations of the United Kingdom Patent Office are not the workings of a national government any more than the practices of the US Mail are directed from the Oval Office. But 'ownership' of intellectual property in something, including a human embryo, does not necessarily imply other instances of ownership. If a biotech company had patents on every cell in my body and every gene in my genome it would not affect my humanity, nor yet my civil, political and moral rights one jot or title. I would not thereby be a slave to the biotech company nor yet in any sense personally 'owned'. This is surely scare mongering. For Rifkin to invoke the parallel with slavery seems to imply both a very shaky understanding of intellectual property issues or a high degree of panic.

In any event the panic is premature. In the United Kingdom, The Patents Act 1977[15] has been amended by the introduction of Schedule A2. Schedule A2 was introduced as part of a set of amendments to the UK Act, which came into force on 28 July 2000, and which were intended to implement EU Directive 98/44/EC on biotechnological inventions.

Schedule A2 provides, *inter alia*, as follows:

1. An invention shall not be considered unpatentable solely on the ground that it concerns –

    (a) a product consisting of or containing biological material; or
    (b) a process by which biological material is produced, processed or used.

2. Biological material which is isolated from its natural environment or produced by means of a technical process may be the subject of an invention even if it previously occurred in nature.

3. The following are not patentable inventions –

(a) the human body, at the various stages of its formation and development, and the simple discovery of one of its elements, including the sequence or partial sequence of a gene;

(b) processes for cloning human beings;

(c) processes for modifying the germ line genetic identity of human beings;

And as to Rifkin's final rhetorical flourish:

> And, if cloned human embryos are, in fact, considered to be human inventions, then what becomes of our notion of God, the creator? What will future generations say when their children ask, where do babies come from? Will they say they are the inventions of scientists and the property of life science companies?

Here I must confess that I for one would feel that future generations would have a better grasp of reality if they have a biological and social explanation of where children come from, a socio-legal explanation of who their parents are (progenitors are something else), and an ethical account of how they and their parents should be considered. And as to the question 'what becomes of our notion of God the creator?' I hope this notion goes the way of all other superstitions; notions that are totally without foundation and are moreover manifestly implausible.

Let us turn now to some very banal objections to cloning that have not been given separate attention so far in this book and treat them with the brevity they doubtless deserve.[16]

Cloning is unnatural. It is sometimes argued that cloning is unethical because it is unnatural. However, 'nature' produces clones both in the vegetable and animal world, and as is well known, humans may give birth to 'twins' (which are genetically identical, if they are monozygotic) by means of natural reproduction. Nature and the natural are of themselves morally neutral; sometimes they do good and are to be approved of, when people are brimming with natural health and vitality for example, or when nature serves us up a sumptuous sunset. Contrariwise, nature can deliver fire, pestilence, disease, pain and premature death. Here we are less likely to accord moral or indeed any other sort of approval.

Humans should not 'play God'. Some always object when humans seem to be aspiring to 'play God'. However, people do not use the objection of 'playing God' in any consistent or even coherent way. We interfere with the course of nature all the time. The whole practice of medicine, for example, may not inappropriately be described as one of our comprehensive attempts to interfere in the course of nature, in that it tries to prevent or alter things that naturally occur, namely illness, disease, injury and premature death. This is playing God if anything is, and yet people use the objection that we should not be 'playing God' only when they refer to interventions of which they disapprove. Of course, they would need to explain why a particular interference is unjustifiable whereas others are not, and unless they provide such an explanation their objection cannot be taken seriously. In short, if it is supposed that we ought not to play God a number of other assumptions must be made. The first is that God has a monopoly of the role (or maybe also that there is only one God), the second is that she is doing a good job (or a better one than we would do) and the third is that God's will is displayed in the operation of 'nature' unmediated by human interference. All these are big and unwarranted assumptions.[17]

We should not produce 'designer children'. As just noted it is sometimes argued that deliberate intervention in the natural process of procreation is an unethical interference with the process of nature. The claim is that it is ethical to let nature run its course, rather then deliberately deciding which characteristics a human being will have. This claim is often combined with the claim that human beings have a 'right to chance', that is, a right to be born 'out of the blind possibilities of nature', rather than of the parents' decisions. A number of philosophers, however, have asked whether it is true that random chance is certainly and always better than deliberate choice.[18] If the moral superiority of 'letting nature run its course' were to be accepted, no medical intervention, nor any other intervention in the course of nature or the natural world of whatever sort (agriculture, for example), would be justifiable. There is also a paradoxical side to this appeal to the random genetic combinations produced by sexual reproduction. If the genome to be cloned is healthy and it might be proved that the child will be healthy, then would it be responsible to go in for the sort of genetic Russian roulette involved in sexual reproduction when a 'tried and tested' genome could be utilised with known susceptibilities to genetic illness and good predictive profile as to life expectancy and future genetically influenced illness?

Cloning commodifies children. One of the worries is that if cloning becomes a reproductive option, this would mean that parents 'may buy' their children. This argument, however, is one against commodifying children, rather than against cloning. Besides, having children in other ways, for example adoption, surrogacy and IVF, may also be costly. If the objection against reproductive cloning is that it would cost money, then the same objection should be raised against the other reproductive methods just mentioned. However, this raises a larger question as to whether or not there is anything wrong with commodifying children so long as this is not the only thing done with them. Problems with this version of the argument concerning instrumentalisation were considered in the previous chapter.

Creating twins a generation apart may have unpredictably bad consequences. The psychosocial consequences of introducing cloning among the ways of having children are unpredictable. But unpredictability is inherent in any procreation and unless serious irreversible harm for the child, or for all parties, will likely result, the argument of unpredictability is arguably not sufficient to deny *a priori* the procedure. It is instead a good reason to investigate the likely consequences at a psychological and social level, and 'the best way' of preparing a child for knowledge about the way in which s/he was brought into the world.

With 'reproductive cloning' someone may create copies of Hitler or create armies of soldiers to establish a universal dictatorship. This objection is based on the mistaken idea, probably spread by fiction, that offspring resulting from the implantation of an embryo derived by CNR would be identical, in terms of personality, inclinations and values, to the nucleus donor. This view is scientifically unfounded and based on a gross misunderstanding of the way character and personality are formed in an individual, and, ultimately, neglects the fundamental importance of environmental factors and the interplay between such factors and genes in the development of personal identity. As to using cloning for the creation of subservient armies of soldiers, we need to take into consideration this rather fantastic scenario only because it is so often mentioned.[19] The utility of CNR for creating armies is minimal. First, despots would have to wait to breed a new army for let us say 16 to 18 years following the initiation of any programme, and despots usually are not that patient. Second, normal breeding will do the job quite as well without going to the extra expense, risk and trouble of using cloning technology. It might be tempting to believe that all this is worth it given that through cloning the despot will have an army of automatons, but there is no evidence nor any reason to suppose that cloning has any affect on free will or autonomy of individuals.

Genetic enhancement. It is sometimes said that cloning could be used for genetic enhancement of human beings, but this idea rests on a simple mistake. Cloning only repeats an existing genome, and does not enhance it. Contrast normal sexual reproduction, which may enhance the gene pool through a lucky accidental combination of genes (or, unlucky, for those who believe genetic enhancement to be a bad thing).

We will now turn to the one argument that seems to have some importance and force in urging caution when contemplating human reproductive cloning

2. SAFETY
Cloning is 'untested and unsafe'

The one decent argument against cloning that does command respect is the claim that in the current state of the art cloning would be likely to result in a high failure rate in pregnancy and an unacceptably high rate of birth defects and genetic abnormalities. There are also persistent fears that clones may have a shorter than average life expectancy. For example, in the case of Dolly, the first cloned mammal, only one clone was successfully produced after 277 attempts.[20]

But embryo wastage *per se* cannot be an objection to

reproductive cloning, at least for anyone who accepts natural reproduction. Approximately 80% of embryos perish in natural reproduction. But not only is natural reproduction inefficient, it is also unsafe. Around 3–5% of babies born have some abnormality. Natural reproduction not only involves the foreseeable and unavoidable creation of some embryos which will die, but also some embryos which will go on to become very disabled human beings. Many embryos are created so genetically abnormal that they cannot survive. They miscarry or spontaneously abort. But some survive only to die as grossly deformed babies. The branch of medicine known as 'teratology', literally 'the study of monsters' bears witness to the problems inherent in natural reproduction, where babies can be born with missing limbs, missing brain, with two heads or where twins can be joined together with two bodies sometimes sharing one head. These used to be referred to in medical literature as 'monstrous births'.

It is clear then that natural sexual reproduction is a method that has a significant risk of failure, death and abnormality. It is however not immediately ruled out as unnaceptably unsafe or 'untested' on this account. Indeed it is well tested and remains unsafe. Natural reproduction is of course also dangerous for the mother. It is well established that carrying a child to term is more dangerous for the mother than early abortion and much more dangerous than not having a child at all.

Cloning then is associated with high rates of embryonic loss and birth abnormalities.[21] The strongest and one of the commonest objections to reproductive cloning is that it is unsafe.[22] As Catholic Archbishop George Pell[23] put it in the *Sunday Telegraph* in Australia in 2001, 'The process used to create Dolly the sheep and other clones has involved a disastrous number of miscarried and monster lambs.'

But things are worse than this from the perspective of objections to human reproductive cloning on the grounds that it is unsafe. Although normal sexual reproduction has a death rate of 80% and an abnormality rate of 3–5% of all live births, this is thought to be lower than that for human reproductive cloning. We do not know yet whether this is correct because figures for cloning are extrapolated from a very few animal cases and there are no data on human cloning. But let's suppose this proves right and that human reproductive cloning would have a significantly higher failure rate than sexual reproduction overall. Would this be a sufficiently powerful argument against permitting human reproductive cloning?

Certainly it might constitute a good moral reason not to use cloning as the reproductive technology of choice, nor for routine reproduction. However, for those who can only have the children they seek through assisted reproduction this might not be a sufficiently powerful moral reason either for those would-be parents to forgo cloning nor for society to prevent them the freedom to access the technology if they choose.

Remember that family histories and genetic testing demonstrate that some individuals or couples have a much higher than average risk of genetic disease or abnormality. While such individuals or families are often counselled about the risks they are never (so far) prevented from attempting to have children at much higher risk of abnormality if they so choose. Thus we accept that the desire to have children genetically related to oneself can justify both running a much higher risk of genetic disease or abnormality or, in some cases, the certainty of such disease or abnormality. It is thus clear that even very enhanced risk or certainty, while widely accepted as a good reason for not having children is not accepted as a justification for preventing high risk individuals or families from procreating if they so choose.

One very important conclusion follows from this discussion. It is that for those who accept natural reproduction, there is no objection in principle to reproductive cloning on grounds of inefficiency or lack of safety, the issue is one of degree of safety or possibly of whether or not there are, in any given case, better acceptable alternatives. Even if attempts at reproductive cloning involve the loss of many embryos which will perish in early embryonic development and also involves the creation of other embryos which will become grossly deformed human beings, this is no different from natural reproduction. Both natural reproduction and human reproductive cloning are relevantly similar activities from the point of view of their moral character – the ethics of the respective activities.[24]

This is a striking conclusion. Acceptance of natural reproduction entails acceptance of reproductive cloning, at least from the perspective of the safety and efficiency of the practice.

Five

Thus far we have examined human reproductive cloning, its impact and the arguments for and against permitting clones to be produced. Admittedly we have concentrated on a critical examination of the arguments against and found all of them wanting. By default, cloning for reproductive purposes seems justified, certainly the arguments for banning it are entirely without merit. Whether or not it is to be enthusiastically welcomed is of course a different matter. We must now look at so-called therapeutic cloning where cloned embryos are produced, not for reproductive purposes but as sources of cells, tissue and possibly organs for research, therapy and transplantation.

WHAT IS THERAPEUTIC CLONING?

So-called therapeutic cloning involves the cloning of an embryo to make the cells, tissue or organs of that embryo compatible with a proposed recipient. The methods whereby this might be achieved have been reviewed in the Introduction to this book.

Stem cell research and therapy

For the remainder of this discussion of therapeutic cloning I will concentrate on its role in the creation and use of stem cells for research and therapy. Stem cells are the most likely use of therapeutic cloning for the foreseeable future and a massive research effort is being deployed to encourage the fruit-bearing potential of this research.[1]

To explore the ethics of therapeutic cloning I will advance one ethical principle, which has not, as yet, received the attention which its platitudinous character would seem to merit.[2] If found acceptable, this principle would permit the beneficial use of any embryonic or fetal tissue which would, by default, be lost or destroyed. More importantly I will make two appeals to consistency or to 'parity of reasoning' which I believe show that no one who either has used, or intends to use sexual reproduction as their means of procreation,[3] nor indeed anyone who has unprotected heterosexual intercourse, nor anyone who finds in vitro fertilization (IVF) acceptable, nor anyone who believes that abortion is ever permissible, can consistently object on principle[4] to human embryo research nor to the use of embryonic stem cells for research or therapy.

This chapter will have four parts. I will begin by simply reviewing the range of ethical issues raised by human embryo stem cell (HESC) research or therapy; I will then examine why human stem cells are so important; third, I will review the current state of social and regulatory policy on stem cells; and finally I will say some positive things about the ethics of HESC research and therapy.

1. WHAT ARE THE ETHICAL ISSUES?

The ethical aspects of human stem cell research raise a wide variety of controversial and important issues. Many of these issues have to do with the different sources of stem cells. In principle stem cells can be obtained from adults, from umbilical cord blood, from fetal tissue and from embryonic tissue. Clearly there are widely differing views as to the ethics of sourcing stem cells in these four different ways. For the moment there is general consensus that embryos are the best source of stem cells for therapeutic purposes but this may of course change as the science develops. Then there is the question of whether or not embryos or fetuses may be deliberately produced in order to be sources of stem cells, whether or not they are also intended to survive stem cell harvesting and grow into healthy adults.

The European Group on Ethics, which advises the European Parliament, is one of the few to have highlighted the women's rights issues that arise here, and in particular we should bear in mind that women, as the most proximate sources of embryonic and fetal material and hence also of cord blood, may be under special pressures and indeed risks if these are to be the sources of stem cells.

There are issues of free and informed consent, both of donors and recipients, the responsibility of accurate risk–benefit assessment, and particular attention needs to be paid to appropriate ethical standards in the conduct of research on human subjects. There are issues concerning the anonymity of the donors and security and safety of cell banks and of the confidentiality and privacy of the genetic information as well as the tissue they contain. Finally there are issues of commerce and remuneration for those taking part and of the transport and security of human tissue and genetic material and information across frontiers both within the EU and worldwide. All of these issues are important but most of them have received extensive discussion over the past few years. For this reason I shall not look in detail at these issues.

Before considering the ethics of such use in detail we

need to understand the possible therapeutic and research uses of stem cells and, equally, the imperatives for research and therapy. These we reviewed in Chapter 1.

2. WHY EMBRYONIC STEM CELLS?

Embryonic stem cells were first grown in culture as recently as February 1998 by James A. Thomson of the University of Wisconsin. In November of that year Thomson announced in *Science* that such human ES cells formed a wide variety of recognisable tissues when transplanted into mice, and these properties of stem cells, to form almost any tissue or bodily system coupled with their regenerative powers, are what makes stem cells such a promising therapeutic tool.

As we noted earlier, stem cells then might eventually enable us not only to grow tailor-made human organs which, using cloning technology of the type that produced Dolly the sheep, could be made individually compatible with their designated recipients. In addition to tailor-made organs or parts of organs, such as heart-valves, for example, it may be possible to use ES cells to colonise damaged parts of the body, including the brain, and to promote the repair and re-growth of damaged tissue. These therapeutic possibilities provide powerful moral reasons to pursue stem cell research.

Immortality

We have already noted (in Chapter 2) the immortalising potential of cloning. Here we should remind ourselves of the possibility of therapies that would extend life, perhaps even to the point at which humans might become in some sense 'immortal'.[5] This, albeit futuristic, dimension of stem cell research raises important issues that are worth serious consideration. Many scientists[6] now believe that death is not inevitable and that the process whereby cells seem to be programmed to age and die is a contingent 'accident' of human development which can in principle and perhaps in fact be reversed[7] and part of that reversal may flow from the regenerative power of stem cells. I have discussed immortality at length elsewhere[8] but we should, before turning to the ethics of stem cell research and therapy, note one important possible consequence of life extending procedures.

Human evolution and species protection

HESC research in general, but the immortalising properties of such research in particular, raises another acute question. If we become substantially longer lived and healthier, and certainly if we transformed ourselves from 'mortals' into 'immortals' we would have changed our fundamental nature. One of the common defining characteristics of a human being is our mortality. Indeed in English we are 'mortals' persons; not 'immortals' or Gods, demi-gods or devils. Is there then any moral reason to stay as we are simply because it is 'as we are'? Is there something sacrosanct about the human life form? Do we have moral reasons against further evolution whether it is 'natural' Darwinian evolution, or evolution determined by conscious choice?

One choice that may confront us is as to whether or not to attempt treatments that might enhance human functioning, so-called 'enhancement therapies'. For example, it may be that because of their regenerative capacities stem cells inserted into the brain to repair damage might in a normal brain have the effect of enhancing brain function. Again it would be difficult if the therapies are proved safe in the case of brain damaged patients to resist requests for their use as enhancement therapies. What after all could be unethical about improving brain function? We don't consider it unethical to choose schools on the basis of their (admittedly doubtful) claims to achieve this, so why would a more efficient method seem problematic?[9]

Marx famously said, 'the purpose of philosophy is not to understand the world but to change it'. Perhaps the purpose of genetics[10] is not to understand humanity but to change it. We should not of course attempt to change human nature for the worse and we must be very sure that in making any modifications we would in fact be changing it for the better, and that we can do so safely, without unwanted side-effects. However, if we could change the genome of human beings, say by adding a new manufactured and synthetic gene sequence which would protect us from most major diseases and allow us to live on average 25% longer with a healthy life throughout our allotted time, I for one, would want to benefit from this and I have not been able to find an argument against so doing that is even worth citing for rebuttal. In the West human beings now do live on average 25% longer than we did 100 years ago but this is usually cited as an unmitigated advantage of 'progress'. It is not widely regretted, there is no wailing and gnashing of teeth; why would regrets or fears be appropriate if a further health gain could be obtained only by species modification or 'directed' evolution? The point is sometimes made that so long as humans continued to be able to procreate after any modifications, which changed our nature, we would still be, in the biological sense, members of the same species. But the point is not whether we remain members of the same species in some narrow biological sense but whether we have changed our nature and perhaps with it our conception of normal species functioning.

3. STEM CELL RESEARCH AND SOCIAL POLICY[11]
The United Kingdom's welcome for stem cell research

On 22 January 2001 the United Kingdom became the first country, certainly in Europe, to approve human embryonic stem cell (HESC) research, albeit with what the government described as 'adequate safeguards'. The United Kingdom Government had set up an 'expert group' under the Chief Medical Officer (CMO's Expert Group) and this group finally reported in June 2000. In August 2000, the Government published its response[12] broadly welcoming the report and accepting all of its major recommendations. These recommendations were the subject of a free vote in both houses of the United Kingdom Parliament and this vote was overwhelmingly for approval of stem cell research and so-called 'therapeutic cloning'. The CMO's Expert Group relied for such argument mainly on the consistency of such research with embryo research already permitted and well established in the United Kingdom under The Human Fertilisation and Embryology Act 1990 and the regulation of research under that Act by the Human Fertilisation and Embryology Authority (the HFEA). Basically, under that Act research on embryos is permitted to investigate problems of infertility and other limited purposes. Now the list of permitted purposes is extended to include human embryonic stem cell research.

The UK Government's policy on stem cells suffered a reverse when a legal action brought by the Pro-Life Alliance succeeded, on 15 October 2001, in getting a declaration that cloning by cell nuclear substitution was outside the terms of the HFE Act 1990. This was because that Act had foolishly and erroneously defined an embryo as 'the product of fertilisation' which of course embryos produced by 'the Dolly method' are not, unless, because they use a cell nucleus produced by fertilisation when the original organism was conceived, the relevant act of fertilisation can be displaced a generation. However, the Pro-Life Alliance lost their case on appeal and emergency legislation rushed through the UK Parliament has banned reproductive cloning, the Government repeating the unsupported[13] claim that human reproductive cloning was 'ethically unacceptable'.

Before addressing 'head on' the ethics of stem cells research as I see it, it is important to place stem cell research in a European and world perspective. There are few comprehensive legal or regulatory frameworks for stem cell research throughout the European Union. Many countries are without any legislation and where laws are in place, they range from an absolute prohibition on embryo research[14] to the permissibility of the creation of embryos for research purposes.[15] This diversity of opinion is a reflection of existing cultural and religious differences. The strength of feeling in some countries regarding embryo research makes even compromise positions difficult to achieve. Governments have to balance strongly held beliefs regarding the moral status of the embryo and fears of instrumentalisation against the promise of remarkable advances in the treatment of disease. There are conflicting duties between state responsibility for the health of their populations and the protection of their moral sensibilities.

The position of European Union countries

In most countries there is a parallel between the permissibility of embryo research and the permissibility of abortion. Ireland is the only EU country whose constitution affirms the right to life of the unborn where this right is equal to that of the mother[16] although it is unclear whether this constitutional right applies from fertilisation or implantation. Despite the constitutional wording, abortion is legitimate if the life of the mother is in immediate danger. Rape, incest or fetal abnormalities are no justification. There is a tension between this attitude and the European Court of Justice decision that abortion constitutes a medical service within the meaning of the European Treaties and that any limitation on the provision of such services by a member state was a matter for the EU rather than Irish law.[17] Ireland had to negotiate special provisions in the Maastricht Treaty in order to maintain their anti-abortion measures. Many applicant countries which have bans or restrictions on abortions, such as Poland, Slovakia, Lithuania, Hungary, Slovenia, the Czech Republic and Malta, may have to do the same.

Belgium and The Netherlands conduct embryo research without a framework of legislation. Portugal, where abortion is illegal except in cases of rape or for serious medical reasons, and banned regardless after the 12th week, has no legislation but no research. It is banned in Austria, Germany and even France, but the latter allows 'the study of embryos without prejudicing their integrity'[18] and pre-implantation diagnosis. The Spanish constitution offers protection only to the in vitro viable embryo; their criteria for viability leaves out spare embryos.[19] Embryo research is permissible under specified conditions in Finland, Spain and Sweden. The most liberal research conditions are to be found in the UK, where even the creation of embryos for research purposes has been legal since the 1990 Human Fertilisation and Embryology Act came into force. The legal situation in nine European countries is either under review or being revised or amended.

For those countries, and the ones with no legislation at all, the situation may be guided by international regulations.

The United States position

The United States seems to share some of Germany's hypocrisy and indecision on this issue. Ten states have passed laws regulating or restricting research on human embryos, fetuses or unborn children, and at federal level funding is prohibited to support any research in which embryos are destroyed. But as we shall see later, this federal prohibition is ominously restrictive and would seem to condemn a number of other practices as well.[20]

International guidelines

International guidelines provide little clarity specifically on human embryo research. Apart from the wide international agreement on the prohibition of human reproductive cloning, agreements at European level have left the permissibility of particular research to the discretion of each member state. There are few guidelines, but if research is authorised by a member state then respect for human dignity requires an appropriate regulatory framework and the provision of guarantees 'against risks of arbitrary experimentation and the instrumentalisation of embryos'. Both Italy and Greece rely upon the Council of Europe's Convention of Human Rights and Biomedicine, Article 18.[21] This stipulates only two conditions: a prohibition on producing embryos for research purposes and the adoption of rules which are designed to ensure adequate protection of embryos. Not all countries have ratified this convention. Human cloning was also banned by the Charter of Fundamental Rights of the European Union in December 2000, as are eugenic practices; but, surprisingly it does not comment explicitly on embryo research.[22] The European Parliament has stated its opposition both to therapeutic cloning and to the creation of spare embryos. Subsequently the European Group of Ethics in Science and New Technologies to the European Commission, while advocating the allocation of a community budget to research on spare embryos from IVF treatment, confirmed the position that it considered the creation of embryos from donated gametes for research purposes ethically unacceptable and 'deemed premature' therapeutic cloning.[23] Those countries which have commissioned an exploration of the issues from their National Ethics Committees or similar bodies provide an insight into the problems of achieving consistency of legislation.

Consistency of legislation

There are many problems regarding the consistency of legislation throughout the EU countries. There often exists a constitutional right to freedom of research and a responsibility to ensure the health of their citizens. Again Germany is an interesting illustration of the paradoxes stem cell research has generated in Europe. Abortion is technically illegal in Germany but women are not penalised provided they receive counselling at a state approved centre which may then issue them with a certificate.[24] So there is a situation where abortion is permissible for a variety of reasons, where the abortion pill RU-486 is available,[25] but where research on embryos is prohibited.

Germany also provides a constitutional right to freedom of research at individual and institutional level and a constitutional duty for the state to protect the life and health of its citizens.[26] This was a consideration for many countries, which debated the ethics of this research. Germany, like the US opted for a compromise position when the Federal Parliament voted to permit limited import of ES cell lines created before 30 January 2002, while maintaining a ban on their derivation within German laboratories.[27] For France, where embryo research is also prohibited, the ethics committee struggled with the fact that prohibition had halted embryonic stem cell research when the therapeutic possibilities make it very desirable. The law is currently under review there and supporters of embryonic stem cell research pointed out that a 'duty of solidarity' with individual suffering prohibits any attempt to stop research.[28] There were pragmatic considerations in the acknowledgment that this research will continue elsewhere and if it produces the results it promises it was considered that French researchers would have no choice but to pursue it anyway.[29] The dilemma now is whether to legislate directly and have safeguards which reflect the sensibilities of French society. The French also raise the concern that improved technical skills in IVF will lead to a decrease in the number of spare embryos. Their ethics committee recommends that the question of oocyte extraction and culture will need to be dealt with explicitly by law to prevent any risk of creating a market situation which would put psychological pressure on women.[30]

Benefiting from evil?

Nations whose constitution (or for that matter democratic will) provides for freedom of research and imposes an obligation on the state to protect the lives and health of citizens and which have outlawed stem cell research may face an agonising dilemma should embryonic stem cell research produce a therapeutic success. They will have to decide whether or not to make the resulting therapy available to their citizens, thereby risking the charge of exploiting and benefiting from the wickedness of others or face the unhappy prospect of watching their citizens die while those of other countries receive treatment. Of course in reality this will not quite be the dilemma since many citizens will seek treatment abroad; but the poor, as ever, are most likely to suffer from such a policy.[31]

The Italian National Bioethics Committee was split on the permissibility of creating embryos for research, a split grounded in the status of the embryo. Some members thought even the use of cryogenically frozen embryos, of which there is a considerable surplus, was not ethically justifiable as respect for human beings prevents instrumental use of these embryos.[32] Those who were in favour of research mentioned the additional consideration of the autonomy of women and couples in deciding to donate their eggs and on the fate of their non-implanted embryos.[33] Despite the legal and constitutional issues and the concerns of pragmatism and consistency, the status of the embryo is a continuous sticking point in the attempt to guide social policy.

4. THE ETHICS OF STEM CELL RESEARCH

Stem cell research is of ethical significance for three major reasons:

(1) The first is that it will for the foreseeable future involve the use and sacrifice of human embryos.
(2) The second is that because of the regenerative properties of stem cells, stem cell therapy may always be more than therapeutic – it may involve the enhancement of human functioning and indeed the extension of human lifespan.

(3) Finally, so-called therapeutic cloning, the use of cell nuclear replacement (CNR) to make the stem cells clones of the genome of their intended recipient, involves the creation of cloned pluripotent and possibly totipotent cells, which some people find objectionable.

Elsewhere I have discussed in detail the ethics of genetic enhancement[34] and the ethics of cloning has been the subject of the earlier chapters of this book. We have noted above the immortalising potential of stem cell research. In this chapter I will concentrate on objections to the use of embryos and fetuses as sources of stem cells.

Since currently the most promising source of stem cells for research and therapeutic purposes is either aborted fetuses or pre-implantation embryos, their recovery and use for current practical purposes seems to turn crucially on the moral status of the embryo and the fetus. A number of recent indications are showing promise for the recovery and use of adult stem cells. It was reported recently that Catherine Verfaillie[35] and her group at the University of Minnesota had successfully isolated adult stem cells from bone marrow and that these seemed to have pluripotent properties (capable of development in many ways but not in all and not capable of becoming a new separate creature) like most HES cells. At about the same time *Nature Online* also published a paper from Ron McKay at NIH showing the promise of embryo derived cells in the treatment of Parkinson's disease.[36]

This indicates the importance of pursuing both lines of research in parallel. The dangers of abjuring embryo research in the hope that adult stem cells will be found to do the job adequately is highly dangerous and problematic for a number of reasons. The first is that we do not yet know whether adult cells will prove as good as embryonic cells for therapeutic purposes; at the moment there is simply much more accumulated data and much more therapeutic promise from HES cells. The second is that it might turn out that adult cells will be good for some therapeutic purposes and HES cells for others. Third, we already know that you can modify or replace virtually any gene in human ES cells, but whether this will also be true of adult stem cells has yet to be established. Finally it would be an irresponsible gamble with human lives to back one source of cells rather than another and to make people wait and possibly die while what is still the less favoured source of stem cells is further developed. This means that the ethics of HESC is still a vital and pressing problem and cannot for the foreseeable future be by-passed by concentration on adult stem cells.

Stem cells from early embryos

It is possible to remove cells from early pre-implantation embryos without damage to the original embryo. This may be one solution to the problem of obtaining embryonic stem cells. However, if the cells removed are totipotent (capable of becoming literally any part of the creature including the whole creature) and if moreover they are capable of deciding until the cell mass achieves sufficient cells for autonomy – the ability to implant successfully and continue to grow to maturity,[37] then they are in effect separate zygotes, they are themselves 'embryos' and so must be protected to whatever extent embryos are protected. If, however, such cells are merely pluripotent, then they could not be regarded as embryos and their use would presumably not offend those who regard the embryo as sacrosanct. Unfortunately it is not at present possible to tell in advance whether a particular cell is totipotent or simply pluripotent. This can only be discovered for sure retrospectively by observing the cells capabilities.

I will now set out one ethical principle that I believe must be added to the central principles cited in guiding our approach to human ES cell research and raise two issues of the consistency of attitudes and judgements about stem cell research with other practices and treatments used and considered acceptable (albeit with qualifications) in not only the EU but indeed in the world at large.

The two issues of consistency I wish to raise are:

(1) Consistency of stem cell research with what is regarded as acceptable and ethical with respect to normal sexual reproduction.
(2) Consistency with attitudes to and moral beliefs about abortion and assisted reproduction.

The ethical principle that I believe we all share and which applies to the use of embryos in stem cell research is the principle of waste avoidance (see below) which assumes that it is right to benefit people if we can, wrong to harm them and states that faced with the opportunity to use resources for a beneficial purpose when the alternative is that those resources are wasted, we have powerful moral reasons to avoid waste and do good instead. I will start with consideration of the first requirement of consistency.

1. LESSONS FROM SEXUAL REPRODUCTION

Let us start with the free and completely unfettered liberty to establish a pregnancy by sexual reproduction without any 'medical' assistance. What are people and societies who accept this free and unfettered liberty committing themselves to? What has a God who has ordained natural procreation committed herself to?[38]

We now know that for every successful pregnancy which results in a live birth many, perhaps as many as five,[39] early embryos will be lost or 'miscarry' (although these are not perhaps 'miscarriages' as the term is normally used because this sort of very early embryo loss is almost always entirely unnoticed.) Many of these embryos will be lost because of genetic abnormalities but some would have been viable. Many people believe that because perhaps a large proportion of these embryos are not viable this somehow makes their sacrifice irrelevant. But those who believe that the embryo is morally important do not usually believe that this importance applies only to healthy embryos. Those who accept the moral importance of the embryo would be no more justified in discounting the lives of unhealthy embryos than those who accept the moral importance of adult humans would be in discounting the lives of the sick or of persons with disability.

How are we to think of the decision to attempt to have a child in the light of these facts? One obvious and inescapable conclusion is that God and/or nature has ordained that 'spare' embryos be produced for almost every pregnancy, and that most of these will have to die in order that a sibling embryo can come to birth. Thus the sacrifice of embryos seems to be an inescapable and inevitable part of the process of procreation. It may not be intentional sacrifice, and it may not attend every pregnancy, but the loss of many embryos is the inevitable consequence of the vast majority (perhaps all) pregnancies. For everyone who knows the facts, it is conscious, knowing and therefore deliberate sacrifice; and for everyone, regardless of 'guilty' knowledge, it is part of the true description of what they do in having or attempting to have children.

We may conclude that the production of spare embryos, some of which will be sacrificed, is not unique to ART; it is an inevitable (and presumably acceptable, or at least tolerable?) part of all reproduction.

Both natural procreation and ART involve a process in which embryos, additional to those which will actually become children, are created only to die. I will continue to call these 'spare' embryos in each case. If either of these processes is justified it is because the objective of producing a live healthy child is judged worth this particular cost. The intentions of the actors, appealed to in the frequently deployed but fallacious doctrine of double effect[40] are not here relevant. What matters is what the agents knowingly and voluntarily bring about. That this is true can be seen by considering the following example.

Suppose we discovered that the use of mobile phones within 50 metres of a pregnant woman resulted in a high probability, near certainty, of early miscarriage. No one would suggest that once this is known, it would be legitimate to continue use of mobile phones in such circumstances on the grounds that phone owners did not intend to cause miscarriages. Any claim by phone users that they were merely intent on causing a public nuisance or, less probably, making telephonic communication with another person and therefore not responsible for the miscarriages would be rightly dismissed. It might of course be the case that we would decide that mobile communications were so important that the price of early miscarriage and the consequent sacrifice of embryos was one well worth paying for the freedom to use mobile phones. And this is, presumably, what we feel about the importance of establishing pregnancies and having children. Mobile phone users of course usually have an alternative method of communication available but we'll suppose they do not.

This example shows the incoherence of the so-called doctrine of double effect. The motives or primary purposes of the phone user are clearly irrelevant to the issue of their responsibility for the consequences of their actions. They are responsible for what they knowingly bring about. The only remaining question is as to whether given the moral importance of what they are trying to achieve (phoning their friends) the consequent miscarriages are a price it is morally justifiable to exact to achieve that end. Here the answer is clearly 'no'. Sometimes proponents of the doctrine of double effect attempt to make proportionality central to the argument. It is not, so it is claimed, the fact that causing miscarriage is not the primary or first intention or effect that matters, but the fact that miscarriage is a serious wrong compared with the benefit of using a mobile phone. However, this is to miss the point of the doctrine of double effect. Proportionality cannot be the issue because the doctrine of double effect was designed to exculpate people from the wrong of intending a forbidden act. The proportionality of the various outcomes cannot speak to the issue of primary or second effects. Only the true account of what the agents wanted to achieve or were 'trying to do', of what the main intention or purpose actually was or is can do that.

However, when we pose the same question about the moral acceptability of sacrificing embryos in pursuance of establishing a successful pregnancy, the answer seems different. My point is that the same issues arise when considering the use of embryos to obtain ES cells. Given the possible therapeutic uses we have reviewed, it would be difficult, I suggest, to regard such uses as other than morally highly significant. Given that decisions to attempt to have children using sexual reproduction as the method (or even decisions to have unprotected intercourse) inevitably create embryos that must die, those who believe having children or even running the risk of conception is legitimate cannot consistently object to the creation of embryos for comparably important moral reasons. The only remaining question is whether or not the use of human embryonic stem cells for therapies designed to save lives and ameliorate suffering are purposes of moral importance comparable to those of attempting to have (or risking the conception of) children by sexual reproduction.

The conscious voluntary production of embryos for research, not as the by-product of attempts (assisted or not) at reproduction is a marginally different case, although some will think the differences important. However, if the analysis so far is correct, then this case is analogous in that it involves the production and destruction of embryos for an important moral purpose. All that remains is to decide what sorts of moral objectives are comparable in importance to that of producing a child. Although some would defend such a position,[41] it would seem more than a little perverse to imagine that saving an existing life could rank lower in moral importance to creating a new life. Assisted reproduction is, for example, given relatively low priority in the provision of health care services. Equally, saving a life that will exist in the future seems morally comparable to creating a future life. In either case the moral quality and importance of the actions and decisions involved and of their consequences seem comparable.

Instrumentalisation

It is important to note that pro-life advocates or Catholics are necessarily acting instrumentally when they attempt to procreate. They are treating the one to four embryos that must be sacrificed in natural reproduction as a conscious (though not intended) means to have a live birth. This is something Catholics certainly and probably most others who hold a 'pro-life' position should not do.

However, the issue is not whether or not Catholics or those who take a 'pro-life' position be permitted to create embryos, which certainly or highly probably will die prematurely, and with whether or not this constitutes reckless endangerment of embryos or even the unjustifiable killing of embryos. Rather, the case of the facts of life, the facts of natural reproduction, show that the creation and destruction of embryos is some-thing that all those who indulge in unprotected intercourse and certainly all those who have children are engaged in. It is not something that only those who use assisted reproduction or those who accept experimentation upon embryos are 'guilty' of. It is a practice in which we are all, if not willing, at least consenting participants, and shows that a certain reverence for or preciousness about embryos is misplaced.

Embryo-sparing ART

It might be said that there is a difference – those who engage in assisted reproduction engage in the destruction of embryos at a greater rate than need be. Those who engage in sex are not engaged in the destruction of embryos at a greater rate than is required for the outcome they seek. It would be inter-esting to know whether, if creating a single embryo by IVF became a reliable technique pro-life supporters would feel obliged to use this method rather than sexual reproduction because of its embryo-sparing advantages. It looks as though there would indeed be a strong moral obligation to abandon natural procreation and use only embryo-sparing ART.

Consider a fictional IVF scenario. A woman has two fertilised eggs and is told it is certain that if she implants both only one will survive but that if she implants only one it will not survive. Would she be wrong to implant two embryos to ensure a successful singleton pregnancy? This example is of course fictional only in terms of the degree of certainty supposed. It is good practice in IVF to implant two or three embryos in the hope of achieving the successful birth of one child. Thus in normal IVF as in normal sexual reproduction the creation and 'sacrifice' of embryos in pursuit of a live child is not only accepted as necessary but is part of the chosen means for achieving the objective. Most people would I believe judge this to be permissible and indeed it is what often happens in successful IVF pregnancies where up to three embryos are implanted in the hope of one live birth. Even in Germany where stem cell research using embryos is currently banned and where legal protections for the embryo are enshrined in the constitution, IVF is permitted and it is usual to implant three embryos in the hope and expectation of achieving no more than a single live birth.

Even if we could accurately predict in advance which embryos would survive and which would not, the ethics would not change. Suppose that for some biological reason there was a condition which required that in order for one embryo to implant it was necessary to introduce a companion embryo which would not, and we could tell in advance which would be which. It is difficult to imagine how or why this fact would alter the ethics of the procedure; it would remain the case that one must die in order that the other survives. If people in this condition wanted ART would we judge it unethical to provide it to them but not to 'normal'

On Cloning

IVF candidates when the 'costs' were the same in each case – namely the loss of one embryo in pursuit of a healthy birth.

It might be objected that the parallel with sexual reproduction is like saying that because we know that road traffic causes thousands of deaths per year, to drive a car is to accept that the sacrifice of thousands of lives in almost every country, for example, is a price worth paying for the institution of motor transport. This might seem a telling analogy showing that we do not willingly accept the inevitable consequences of what we do. There are, of course, many disanalogous features of the purported *reductio ad absurdum* comparison with road deaths. The vast majority of drivers will go all their lives without having an injury causing incident let alone a fatality, and the probability of any individual causing a death once exacerbating factors such as alcohol use and reckless fatigue are taken into account is vanishingly small by any standards and insignificant when compared with the high risk of production of embryos in unprotected sex between fertile partners. However, suppose an individual knew that despite a long driving career without accidents today is the day that either they will surely be involved in a fatal accident and cause someone's death or that the probability of this happening is very high indeed. Would it be conceivable that it might be permissible, let alone ethical, to drive today? And yet that is the situation with normal sexual intercourse, at least for those who regard the embryo as protected.

The natural is not connected to the moral

It is important to be clear about the form of this argument. I am not of course suggesting that because something happens in nature it must be morally permissible for humans to choose to do it. I am not suggesting that because embryos are produced only to die in natural procreation that the killing of embryos must be morally sound. I am saying rather, that if something happens in nature *and* we find it acceptable in nature given all the circumstances of the case, then if the circumstances are relevantly similar it will for the same reasons be morally permissible to achieve the same result as a consequence of deliberate human choice. I am saying that we do as a matter of fact and of sound moral judgement accept the sacrifice of embryos in natural reproduction, because although we might rather not have to sacrifice embryos in order to achieve a live healthy birth, we judge it to be defensible to continue natural reproduction in the light of the balance between the moral costs and the benefits. And if we make this calculation in the case of normal sexual reproduction we should, for the same reasons, make a similar judgement in the case of the sacrifice of embryos in stem cell research.

To take a different but analogous case: if we say that God and/or nature 'approves' of cloning by cell division because of the high rate of natural monozygotic twinning[42] and that therefore the duplication of the human genome is not *per se* unethical, we are not saying that cloning by cell division is ethically unproblematic because it occurs naturally. The intent of the analogy is rather that by pointing out the fact that when natural identical twins are born no one thinks that something terrible has happened, we are reminding ourselves that there is nothing here to regret. That having considered the phenomenon of natural monozygotic twinning we can find nothing reprehensible or regrettable about it – it is the occasion for unmitigated joy or at least moral neutrality. We should therefore, unless we can find a difference, feel the same about choosing deliberately to create twins by this method.[43] If we then object to cloning by a different method, Cell Nuclear Replacement (CNR) objections must obviously be to features that arise uniquely in CNR and cannot simply be to such features as duplication of the human genome. Our acceptance of the natural does not of course apply to naturally occurring premature death, here we do think there is something to regret even if it is 'natural' and inevitable.

Instrumentalisation revisited

Another possible concern[44] involves a version of the instrumentalisation objection which demands that embryos be not produced only to be used for the benefit of others but that, as in sexual reproduction, they should all have some chance of benefiting from a full normal lifespan. In normal sexual reproduction embryos must be created only to die so that a sibling embryo can come to birth. But arguably it is in each embryo's interests that reproduction continues because it is their only chance to be the one that survives. Embryos (if they had rationality) would have a rational motive to participate (albeit passively) in sexual reproduction. By contrast, so it might be claimed, embryos produced specifically for research would not rationally choose to participate for they stand to gain nothing. All research embryos will die and none have a chance of survival. If this argument is persuasive against the production of research embryos it is easily answered by ensuring that the production of research embryos to some appropriate extent have a real chance of survival. One would simply have to produce more embryos than were required for research, randomise allocation to research and ensure that the remainder were implanted with a chance to become persons. To ensure that it was in every embryo's interests to be 'a research embryo' all research protocols permitting the production of research embryos would have to produce extra embryos for implantation. To take a figure at random but one that as it happens mirrors natural reproduction and gives a real chance of survival to all embryos, we could ensure that for every, say 100 embryos needed for research another 10 would be produced for implantation. The 100 embryos would be randomised 90 for research, 10 for implantation, and all would have a chance of survival and an interest in the maintenance of a process which gave them this chance.

The third case here is that of spare embryos that become available for research as a result of an ART programme in which they have been produced and to which they are now superfluous because their 'mother' has now declined for whatever reason to accept more embryos for implantation and has refused consent for their implantation into others. Here it might be suggested that these embryos are also like the research embryos just considered. However, this is not the case. These embryos have had their chance of implantation, but unfortunately for them they have missed out. The fact that now they are irredeemably surplus to requirements for implantation does not show that they always were. These embryos have had their chance of life, their 'motive' for participating in the programme is as strong as in sexual reproduction or randomised research embryos.

Born to die

The force of the sexual reproduction analogy may seem vulnerable to the following claim.[45] It can be said that just as parents are responsible for the deaths of the embryos inevitably produced as a consequence of unprotected intercourse, so also and to the same extent are they responsible for the deaths of the children they actually produce when these children eventually die of old age. This is because in each case the parents have produced a life, which will end at a particular point and that point is in each case out of the parents' control. So if parents are responsible for the deaths of the embryos lost as a result of unprotected intercourse they are also responsible for the deaths of their children lost in old age. In neither case however have the parents been the proximate cause of death but they have caused the life and death cycle. This objection, like the objection from the acceptability of motorised road transport, purports to constitute a *reductio ad absurdum*.

This is a puzzling objection. As we have argued, people accept the necessity of and the justification for producing surplus embryos because they wish to have a baby. Those who judge the embryo to have moral importance comparable to adults or children will have to justify their instrumentalisation of the embryos that are sacrificed to this end.

On the other hand those who think that dying of old age or being given a worthwhile life is a good, will see nothing to justify. The parents are responsible for that life to be sure but they are morally justified in that responsibility and in that the life for which they are responsible has been or is reasonably likely to be a worthwhile life then, unless they have also arranged the death, their responsibilities have been exercised in a way that is both morally and socially appropriate.

The life of their child was in this case neither created nor ended to be a means to the interests of others. It is a good life the creation of which requires no justification and the end of which was neither caused by the parents nor was its timing predictable by them. They therefore have no excuses to make. By contrast the lives of the embryos that must die early are, if those lives are morally important at all, not lives the ending of which is a reasonable price to pay for the life lived.

The United States condemns human reproduction!

Shocked by the idea of any activity that threatens the embryo, the United States Government has adopted the revolutionary strategy of attempting to condemn human reproduction and for good measure has included all unprotected intercourse in this condemnation and to ban all federal support for such activities.

How have our cousins in the United States arrived at this daring and groundbreaking social policy? In the United States, current federal law prohibits the use of federal funds for 'the creation of a human embryo' explicitly for research purposes or, more crucially, for 'research in which a human embryo or embryos are destroyed, discarded or knowingly subjected to the risk of injury or death'.[46] Such law is presumably animated by concern about the morally problematic nature of such actions and also by the idea that federal support in the form (among others) of 'tax dollars', should not be given to activities that a significant number of people find offensive or objectionable. As we have noted, normal sexual reproduction inevitably involves a process in which 'a human embryo or embryos are destroyed or discarded'. It is also incontrovertibly an activity in which 'a human embryo or embryos' are 'knowingly subjected to the risk of injury or death'; at least for anyone who knows the facts of life. The perpetuation of this position seems likely as the incoming United States President George W. Bush had made an election promise never to provide federal support for 'research that involves living human embryos'.

2. CONSISTENCY WITH ATTITUDES TO AND MORAL BELIEFS ABOUT ABORTION AND ASSISTED REPRODUCTION

In most countries of the European Union, and indeed in most countries of the world, abortion is permissible under some circumstances. Usually permissibility is considered greater at very early stages of pregnancy, permissibility waning with embryonic and fetal development. The most commonly accepted ground for abortion (where it is acceptable) is to protect the life and the health of the mother. Sometimes the idea of protection of the life and health of the mother is very broadly and liberally interpreted, as it is in the UK, sometimes the requirement is very strict, demanding real and present danger to the life and health of the mother (Northern Ireland for example). Given that the therapies initially posited for stem cell research – the treatment of Parkinson's disease and the development of tailor-made transplant organs, are all for serious diseases which threaten both life and dramatically compromise health – it is difficult to see how those who think the sacrifice of early embryos for these serious purposes is or could be justified could find principled objections to the use of embryos in other life-saving therapies.[47]

The same is of course true, as we have already noted of assisted reproduction. All in vitro fertilisation involves the creation of spare embryos and all IVF now practised is built on research done on many thousands of embryos. Most countries and most religions accept IVF and its benefits and in doing so accept that spare embryos will be produced only to die. Even Germany which has, as we have noted, an Embryo Protection Act, accepts the practice of implanting up to three embryos in the hope and expectation that at least one will survive. The acceptance of the practice of IVF is necessarily an acceptance that embryos may be created and destroyed for a suitably important moral purpose.

3. THE PRINCIPLE OF WASTE AVOIDANCE

This widely shared principle states that it is right to benefit people if we can, wrong to harm them and that faced with the opportunity to use resources for a beneficial purpose when the alternative is that those resources are wasted, we have powerful moral reasons to avoid waste and do good instead.

The fact that it is surely better to do something good than to do nothing good should be re-emphasised. It is difficult to find arguments in support of the idea that it could be better (more ethical) to allow embryonic or fetal material to go to waste than to use it for some good purpose. It must, logically, be better to do something good than to do nothing good; it must be better to make good use of something than to allow it to be wasted. It must surely be *more* ethical to help people than to help no one. This principle, that other things being equal it is better to do some good than no good, implies that tissue and cells from aborted fetuses should be available for beneficial purposes in the same way that it is ethical to use organs and tissue from cadavers in transplantation.

It does not of course follow from this that it is ethical specially to create embryos for the purposes of deriving stem cells from them. However, as we have seen, there may be problems in objecting to creating embryos for this purpose from people who do not object to the sacrifice of embryos in pursuit of another supposedly beneficial objective, namely the creation of a new human being. Only those who think that it is more important to create new humans that to save existing ones will be attracted to the idea that sexual reproduction is permissible whereas the creation of embryos for therapy is not.

Conclusion

The conclusions of this book are simply stated:

(1) I conclude that human reproductive cloning is in principle both ethical and permissible and that so-called therapeutic cloning is ethical, permissible and indeed mandatory. While there are few pressing moral reasons to pursue human reproductive cloning there are overwhelmingly powerful reasons to pursue therapeutic cloning, stem cell research and other research which therapeutic cloning will augment and probably make much more effective. The reasons for pursuing this research are so strong that it would be unethical not to pursue this research.

(2) I conclude that if there is an issue of human dignity which is engaged by human cloning in any of its forms, it is the huge indignity of permitting the legislative and regulatory agenda to be set by a combination of panic and prejudice. Added to which is the indignity of witnessing an undignified scramble to produce literally any argument, however poor or implausible, so long as it seems to provide some grounds for rejecting cloning.

Many more specific conclusions have been drawn chapter by chapter as the argument has developed. These have often been that we should reject poor arguments against cloning and in favour of caution, and that in the absence of good arguments against cloning or compelling evidence that it will cause harm or that it presents dangers, two considerations have overriding force.

The first is a presumption in favour of liberty. A fundamental principle of the morality of all democratic countries is that human liberty should not be abridged without good cause being shown. Where the liberty in question is trivial or vexatious, or is itself morally dubious or even morally neutral, it is plausible to claim that no harm is done if liberty is sacrificed – particularly where popular support for the limitation of a particular freedom can be demonstrated. However, where a case can be made to the effect that the freedom which has been abridged is not only not trivial, vexatious or morally dubious but rather is itself the expression of or a dimension of something morally significant, then its abridgement becomes a serious matter. We have seen that reproductive cloning is part of reproductive liberty more generally and is therefore certainly a liberty claim of seriousness and importance. Therapeutic cloning, which offers important therapeutic successes, is not only far from trivial but is clearly also required by acceptance of a duty both of beneficence and of non-maleficence.

These two widely accepted and shared moral principles or duties, namely the duty of beneficence (the duty to do good) and the duty of non-maleficence (the obligation to avoid harming others, which includes harms of omission) in combination constitute the second powerful set of reasons we have to reject poor arguments against cloning. Of course there is always some 'small print' and here it follows.

HUMAN REPRODUCTIVE CLONING – SAFETY ISSUES

We have noted the safety issues involved in human reproductive cloning. Because of the present high failure rate and enhanced risk of malformations no sane person would lightly select reproductive cloning as a procreational pathway of choice. Whether these dangers constitute justification for a continued ban on reproductive cloning is however surely doubtful. We do not ban opportunities to procreate to those who, because of genetic or other risk factors have a higher than average chance of failure or of malformations. In these cases we judge counselling and good information to be sufficient and I see no good argument for different principles or a different approach in the case of cloning.

THERAPEUTIC CLONING – SAFETY ISSUES

There is one continuing safety issue for CNR if it is ever to result in cells or tissue that will be transplanted into human beings and that is the provision of a proven safe medium for growing stem cells. Researchers are well aware of this need and the high priority that it has, and there is no question of therapies being tried while this problem remains. However, once this issue is resolved and as therapies come on stream and are adequately tested in the normal ways, there is no doubt that in so far as therapeutic cloning will make cells and tissue safer and more compatible with intended recipients, its use is not simply permissible but mandatory.

We should remind ourselves in closing of the arguments of the introductory chapter to this book. If hopes for stem cell therapy are realised and treatments become available for congestive heart failure, diabetes and other diseases and if, as many believe, tailor-made transplant organs will eventually be possible, then literally millions of people worldwide will be treated using stem cell therapy.

When a possible new therapy holds out promise of dramatic cures we should of course be cautious, if only to avoid raising false hopes of an early treatment; but equally we should, for the sake of all those awaiting therapy, pursue the research that might lead to therapy with all vigour and urgency. To fail to do so would be to deny people who might benefit the possibility of therapy. It would be to condemn millions of people not only to needless delays in searching for a therapy, but it would be to deny them hope. This creates a positive moral duty to pursue research, which offers realistic prospect of therapeutic success.

We cannot rationally or coherently exercise caution or indeed follow the precautionary principle unless we have very accurate foresight into two alternative scenarios. We need to know on the one hand how much harm the proposed research and the proposed therapies might involve, and second, we need to know how much good they will do. We usually know neither of these things. And usually we have no rational basis for determining where the balance of risk and benefit lies. The precautionary principle urges us, irrationally, to give more weight to risks than to benefits. But delay in producing benefit is a real risk to those who might benefit from scientific advance. In such circumstances it is irrational, self-defeating and immoral to give all the weight in our considerations to realistic fears of harm and none to equally realistic prospects of benefit.

Notes

PREFACE

1 See my 'In vitro fertilisation: the ethical issues' in *The Philosophical Quarterly* Vol. 33, No. 132, July 1983.

ONE ON CLONING: AN INTRODUCTION

1 In this section I draw on John Harris and Simona Giordano 'On Cloning', *The Routledge Encyclopedia of Philosophy*, Edward Craig (ed.) Online Edition 2003. I am very much indebted to my colleague Simona Giordano for her important and major contributions to this chapter.

2 Triplets probably occur when the egg splits twice but one of the resulting 'clones' dies. See for example Gary Steinman 'Spontaneous monozygotic quadruplet pregnancy: An obstetric rarity' in *Obstetrics & Gynecology* 1988, p. 866.

3 For the problematic nature of attributing moral significance to early embryos see my *The Value of Life*, Routledge 1985, and 'Stem cells, sex and procreation', *Cambridge Quarterly of Healthcare Ethics*, Vol. 12, No. 4, Fall 2003, pp. 353–372.

4 Since writing this I have been alerted to this possibility by Julian Savulescu – another example of synchronicity in bioethics?

5 Unless of course the nucleus donor is also the egg donor.

6 See http://www.dnapolicy.org/genetics/chronology.jhtml

7 Although Aldous Huxley may have been rather better informed about the science than most through his brother Julian, a leading scientist of the day.

8 Ibid.

9 See Anne McClaren 'The decade of the sheep', *Nature* Vol. 403, 2000, pp. 479–480.

10 In this section and the next I again draw on John Harris and Simona Giordano 'On Cloning', *The Routledge Encyclopedia of Philosophy*, Edward Craig (ed.) Online Edition 2003.

11 DOH (2000) – Department of Health: Stem Cell Research: Medical Progress with Responsibility. A report from the Chief Medical Officer's Expert Group reviewing the potential of developments in stem cell research and cell nuclear replacement to benefit human health, Department of Health, June 2000. (This document provides clear guidelines through the technical and ethical issues surrounding stem cell research in general and contains sections on CNR.)

12 Ibid., p. 26.

13 House of Lords (2002) *Stem Cell Research, Report from the Select Committee*, London: Stationery Office. (Technical, ethical, social and legal issues surrounding stem cell research are analysed in this comprehensive document. Sections on cloning are included.)

14 DOH 2000, p. 26. Note 11 above.

15 Ibid., p. 26.

16 John Harris and Søren Holm 'Extended lifespan and the paradox of precaution' in *The Journal of Medicine and Philosophy*, 2002.

17 N. Ashford et al. Wingspread Statement on the Precautionary Principle, 1998, http://www.gdrc.org/u-gov/precaution-3.html.

18 I must acknowledge that this 'reductio' of the precautionary principle is the invention of Søren Holm.

19 J.A. Thomson et al. *Science* Vol. 282, 6 Nov. 1998. Roger Pedersen, *Scientific American*, April 1999.

20 David J. Mooney and Antonios G. Mikos 'Growing new organs', *Scientific American*, April 1999, pp. 38–43.

21 David K.C. Cooper and Robert P. Lanza, *Xeno: The Promise of Transplanting Animal Organs into Humans*, Oxford University Press, Oxford 2000. Chapters 1 and 2.

22 M.C. De Rijk et al. 'Prevalence of Parkinson's disease in Europe', *Neurology* 54 (11 Suppl 5), pp. S21–23, 2000.

23 A. Schrag et al. 'Cross sectional prevalence survey of idiopathic Parkinson's disease and Parkinsonism in London', *British Medical Journal* Vol. 321 (7252) 1 July 2000, pp. 21–22.

24 http://www.parkinsons.org.uk/docs/

25 Source 'Parkinson's Disease Foundation, Inc. http://www.pdf.org/aboutdisease/overview/imdex.html

26 Ian Wilmut et al. 'Viable offspring derived from fetal and adult mammalian cells', *Nature*, 27 February 1997.

27 See *Cloning Human Beings: Report and Recommendations of the National Bioethics Advisory Commission*, Rockville, MD, June 1997.

28 From President Clinton's weekly radio broadcast reported in *Bioworld Today* Vol. 9. No. 7 Tuesday 13 January 1998. Interestingly the National Bioethics Advisory Commission stated that it was unethical *because* unsafe. Either Clinton misread his advisers' report or decided to add 'morally unacceptable' on top of the fact that it was untested and unsafe rather than simply because it was untested and unsafe.

29 George W. Bush *Remarks by the President on Stem Cell Research*, The White House, 9 August 2001. http://www.whitehouse.gov/news/releases/2001/08/20010809–2.html

30 Reported in *BioCentury, The Bernstein Report on BioBusiness*, 19 January 1998.

31 The European Parliament, Resolution on Cloning, Motion dated 11 March 1997. Passed 13 March 1997.

32 *Government Response to the Recommendations Made in the Chief Medical Officer's Expert Group Report*, August 2000, The Stationery Office Cm 4833.

33 The most reliable recently published article on the subject is S. Macintyre and A. Sooman, *Lancet* 1991, Vol. 338, p. 1151, and ensuing correspondence.

34 Source http://news.bbc.co.uk/1/hi/health/2570503.stm

35 For more on this particular fascination, see my 'Intimations of immortality' in *Science* Vol. 288, No. 5463 p. 59, 7 April 2000. 'Intimations of immortality – the ethics and justice of life extending therapies' in Michael Freeman (ed.) *Current Legal Problems*, Oxford University Press 2002, pp. 65–95.

36 Despite some powerful dissent from Aristotle.

37 I owe this example to Julian Savulescu.

38 See note 10 above.

39 Histocompatible simply means 'compatible tissue'. The key point is that organs be sufficiently similar to avoid dangers of rejection when implanted in a host.

40 See J.M.W. Slack et al. 'The role of fibroblast growth factors in early Xenopus development', in *Biochem. Soc. Symp.* Vol. 62, pp. 1–12.

TWO   HUMAN DIGNITY AND REPRODUCTIVE AUTONOMY

1 See, for example, Gary Steinman 'Spontaneous monozygotic quadruplet pregnancy: An obstetric rarity' in *Obstetrics & Gynecology* 1998, p. 866.

2 I am told (personal communication from Julian Savulescu) that the rate can be as low as one in every 40 births. In the literature I have so far found reference only to a rate of 1:80 births. See Sills et al. 'Human zona pellucida micromanipulation and monozygotic twinning frequency after IVF' in *Human Reproduction*, April 2000, Vol. 15, No. 4, pp. 890–895.

3 Katrien Devolder pointed this out to me. S.N. IVF baby marks 25th anniversary. BBC News, 26 July 2003 (http://news.bbc.co.uk/1/hi/health/3098437.stm). According to the American Society of Reproductive Medicine, 114,000 babies have been born in the United States alone (http://www.cnn.com/2003/HEALTH/parenting/07/25/ivf.anniversary/index.html.).

4 Axel Kahn 'Clone mammals . . . clone man', *Nature*, Vol. 386, 13 March 1997, p. 119.

5 See my 'Is cloning an attack on human dignity', *Nature*, Vol. 387, 19 June 1997, p. 754.

6 *Opinion of the Group of Advisers on the Ethical Implications of Biotechnology to the European Commission* No. 9. 28 May 1997. Rapporteur Dr Anne McClaren.

7 Axel Kahn, *Nature*, Vol. 388, 24 July 1997, p. 320.

8 See Hilary Putnam in Justine Burley ed. *The Genetic Revolution and Human Rights*, Oxford: Oxford University Press, 1999, pp. 1–14. Richard Lewontin 'Confusion about cloning' *The New York Review of Books*, 23 October 1997, pp. 18–23.

9 For Putnam's quotation see his essay note 8 above, pp. 10–11. For mine see my 'Rights and human reproduction' in John Harris and Søren Holm (eds). *The Future of Human Reproduction: Choice and Regulation*, Oxford: Oxford University Press, 1998.

10 Ibid.

11 I realise Putnam says nothing about punishment. But by saying that Nazism might easily follow were cloning permitted, Putnam is certainly giving support to those who would outlaw human cloning.

12 Ibid.

13 My added emphasis.

14 Leaving aside, for the sake of the moral image, the interests of the child.

15 And, for good measure, perhaps we should use legislation to prevent any family having an established religion.

16 Another argument for the surprise factor in cloning!

17 Federico Mayor 'Devaluing the human factor' in *The Times Higher*, 6 February 1998.

18 Robert Winston, *British Medical Journal* Vol. 314 1997, pp. 913–914.

19 See Hilary Putnam note 8 above.

20 It is unlikely that 'artificial' cloning would ever approach such a rate on a global scale and we could, of course, use regulative mechanisms to prevent this without banning the process entirely. I take this figure of the rate of natural twinning from Keith L. Moore and T.V.N. Persaud *The Developing Human* (5th edn), W.B. Saunders, Philadelphia, 1993. The rate mentioned is one per 270 pregnancies.

21 Mitochondrial DNA individualises the genotype even of clones to some extent. The mitochondria are particles of DNA present in each egg cell and are derived from the mother of that egg. They are additional to the 46 chromosomes that make-up the genome which is cloned using nuclear substitution.

22 Although of course there would be implications for criminal justice since clones could not be differentiated by so called 'genetic finger-printing' techniques.

23 David Hume in his *A Treatise of Human Nature* 1738. Contemporary philosophers who have flirted with a similar approach include Stuart Hampshire, see for example his *Morality & Pessimism – The Leslie Stephen Lecture*, Cambridge: Cambridge University Press, 1972, and Bernard Williams in for example his 'Against utilitarianism' in B. Williams and J.J.C. Smart, *Utilitarianism For and Against*, Cambridge: Cambridge University Press, 1973. I first discussed the pitfalls of olfactory moral philosophy in my *Violence and Responsibility* London: Routledge & Kegan Paul, 1980.

24 Mary Warnock, 'Do human cells have rights?', *Bioethics*, Vol. 1, No. 1, January 1987, p. 8.

25 Leon R. Kass 'The wisdom of repugnance' in *The New Republic*, 2 June 1997, pp. 17–26. The obvious erudition of his writing leads to expecta-

tions that he might have found feelings prompted by more promising parts of his anatomy with which to entertain us.

26 In a letter to Humphrey House 11 April 1940. *The Collected Essays, Journalism and Letters of George Orwell* Vol. 1, London: Penguin, Harmondsworth, 1970, p. 583. See my more detailed discussion of the problems with this type of reasoning in *Wonderwoman & Superman: The Ethics of Human Biotechnology*, op. cit. Chapter 2.

27 See note 2 above.

28 Ronald Dworkin *Life's Dominion*, London: Harper Collins, 1993, p. 148. See also John A. Robertson *Children of Choice*, Princeton: Princeton University Press, 1994, especially Chapter 2.

29 Dworkin op. cit., p. 160.

30 Ronald Dworkin *Freedom's Law*, Oxford: Oxford University Press, 1996, pp. 237–238.

31 Ronald Dworkin has produced an elegant account of the way the price we should be willing to pay for freedom might or might not be traded off against the costs. See his *Taking Rights Seriously*, London: Duckworth, 1977, Chapter 10. And his *A Matter of Principle*, Cambridge, MA, 1985, Chapter 17.

32 Ronald Dworkin *Life's Dominion*, pp. 166–167.

33 *State of Washington* et al. *Petitioners v. Glucksberg* et al., *and Vacco* et al, *v. Quill* et al. argued 8 January 1997.

34 Federico Mayor 'Devaluing the human factor', *The Times Higher*, 6 February 1998.

35 John Robertson *Children of Choice*, Princeton: Princeton University Press, 1996, p. 25.

36 John Robertson 'Procreative Liberty in the Era of Genomics', unpublished MS p. 60.

37 Ibid.

38 I talk of the genetic relatedness of families here, but while such talk has some meaning and precise degrees of genetic relatedness can be accurately assessed using genome analysis, we should remember that all humans share approximately 99.90% of their genes with one another and closer relationships involve a very small proportion of the human genome.

39 *The Shorter Oxford English Dictionary*, Clarendon Press, Oxford, 1968.

40 Robertson op. cit., pp. 17–18.

THREE   THE WELFARE OF THE CHILD

1 I thank Charles Erin for incisive comments. Some of the arguments used here were first published in my 'The welfare of the child' in *Health Care Analysis* Vol. 8, No. 1 2000, pp. 27–34

2 *Surrogacy: Review For Health Ministers of Current Arrangements For Payments and Regulation – Report of the Review Team*, The Stationery Office, October 1998. ISBN 0–10–140682–7.

3 Ibid., paras 4.28–4.29.

4 Ibid., para 4.33.

5 See para 4.44.

6 This question of course also has a personal form, which asks: 'What sort of child should I try to bring into being?'

7 Obviously if no decision is taken to bring a child into being, or if a decision is taken to abort an existing embryo or fetus, then no person will exist to be affected.

8 See Derek Parfit *Reasons & Persons*, Oxford: Clarendon Press, 1984, Ch. 16. And Justine Burley and John Harris 'Human cloning and child welfare' in *The Journal of Medical Ethics*, February 1999.

9 Indeed it specifically charges me with this confusion. See para 4.27.

10 Para 4.44.

11 My emphasis.

12 Op. cit., para 4.32.

13 General considerations would here favour the rich, personal considerations would be neutral because different children would result from different policies.

14 Ibid., paras 4.28–4.29.

15 See for example my *Clones, Genes and Immortality*, Oxford: Oxford University Press, 1998. Chapters 1 and 2.

16 Ibid., para 4.33.

17 For a discussion of procreative autonomy see John Harris 'Genes, clones and human rights' in Justine C. Burley (ed.) *The Genetic Revolution and Human Rights: The Amnesty Lectures 1998*, Oxford: Oxford University Press, 1999.

18 *The Brazier Report*, para 4.32.

19 Cambridge University Press, Cambridge 2002. These also formed the basis of her 2003 Reith Lecture Series on BBC Radio 4. I would like to record my thanks to Martin Richards for many of the sources on family relationships.

20 Ibid., pp. 67–68.

21 Ibid. Leon Kass makes similar claims that the troubled psychic identity of a clone 'will be made much worse by the utter confusion of social identity and kinship ties'. He says that cloning radically confounds lineage and social relations, for 'offspring' as for 'parents'. See L.R. Kass 'The wisdom of repugnance', *The New Republic*, 1997, pp. 22–23, note 36.

22 Indeed because children for adoption are a 'scarce resource' would-be adoptive parents usually have to be better than Caesar's wife.

23 I am far from convinced that adoption is a regrettable necessity, but unpacking that idea is a task for another occasion.

24 Ibid., pp. 67–68.

25 Assuming we are convinced it is desirable to do so. I am reminded of the, possibly apocryphal, story concerning James Callaghan, the Labour Prime Minister. He, unique among recent Prime Ministers, had not been to university, and when he was Chancellor of the Exchequer he apparently took extra tuition in economics with an academic at Nuffield College Oxford. The Don was once asked what Callaghan was like as a student and responded – 'Jim Callaghan . . . a very hard man to bamboozle (confuse) but once bamboozled, a very hard man to un-bamboozle!' This trait may not extend to all children however.

26 There is a vast literature on the risks of harm to children from various factors concerning their origins; most of them sceptical about the bad effects of ambiguity, confusion, use of reproductive technologies, adoption, fostering divorce, etc. Here is some of this literature. I am indebted to Susan Golombok and Martin Richards for many of these sources: Susan Golombok and Fiona Tasker: 'Do parents influence the sexual orientation of their children? Findings from a longitudinal study of lesbian families' *Development Psychology* 1996, Vol. 32, No. 1, pp. 3–11. Fiona Tasker, PhD, and Susan Golombok, PhD 'Adults raised as children in lesbian families' *Amer. J. Orthopsychiat.* Vol. 65, No. 2, April 1995. Susan Golombok, Fiona Tasker and Clare Murray 'Children raised in fatherless families from infancy: Family relationships and the socioemotional development of children of lesbian and single heterosexual mothers,' *Child Psychol.* Vol. 38, No. 7, pp. 783–791, 1997. Cambridge University Press. Susan Golombok, Clare Murray, Peter Brinsden and Hossam Abdalla, 'Social versus biological parenting: Family functioning and

socioemotional development of children conceived by egg or sperm donation', *Child Psychiat.* Vol. 40, No. 4, pp. 519–527, 1999, Cambridge University Press. Susan Golombok, Rachel Cook, Alison Bish and Clare Murray 'Families created by the new reproductive technologies: Quality of parenting and social and emotional development of the children', *Child Development* Vol. 66, 1995, pp. 285–298. A. Golombok, R. Brewaeys, M.T. Cook, D. Giavazzi, A. Guerra, E. Mantovani, P. van Hall, Crosignani G. and S. Dexeus 'The European study of assisted reproduction families: family functioning and child development' *Human Reproduction* Vol. 11, No. 10, pp. 2324–2331, 1996. Rachel Cook, PhD, Susan Golombok, PhD, Alison Bish, BSc, and Clare Murray, BSc 'Disclosure of donor insemination: Parental attitudes' *Amer. J. Orthopsychiat* Vol. 65, No. 4, October 1995. R. Cook (2002) 'Villain, hero or masked stranger: ambivalence in transactions with human genetics,' in A. Bainham, S. Day-Sclater and M. Richards (eds) *Body Lore and Laws*, Oxford: Hart Publishing. R. Cook, and S. Golombok (1995) 'A survey of semen donation: phase 2 – the view of donors', *Human Reproduction*, Vol. 10, pp. 951–959. R. Cook 'Donating parenthood: Perspectives on parenthood from surrogacy and gamete donation' in A. Bainham, S. Day-Sclater and M. Richards (eds) *What is a Parent? A Socio-Legal Analysis*, Oxford, Hart Publishing, 1999. S. Franklin and S. McKinnon (2001) *Relative Values: Reconfiguring Kinship Studies*, Durham, NC: Duke University Press. S. Franklin (2001) 'Biologization revisited: kinship theory in the context of the new biologies,' in S. Franklin and S. McKinnon (eds), *Relative Values: Reconfiguring Kinship Studies*, Durham, NC: Duke University Press. M. Freeman (1996) 'The new birth right?' *International Journal of Children's Rights* Vol. 4, pp. 273–297. A. Giddens (1991) *Modernity and Self-Identity: Self and Society in the Late Modern Age*, Cambridge: Polity. S. Golombok, A. Brewaeys, R. Cook et al. (1996) 'The European study of assisted reproduction families' *Human Reproduction* Vol. 11, pp. 2324–2331. S. Golombok, A. Brewaeys, M.T. Giavazzi, et al. (2002) 'The European study of assisted reproduction families: the transition to adolescence' *Human Reproduction* Vol. 17, pp. 830–840. S. Golombok (2002) 'Parenting and contemporary reproductive technologies' in M.H. Barnstein (ed.), *Handbook of Parenting* (2nd edn) Vol. 3, Mahwah, NJ: Erlbaum. E. Blyth, M. Crawshaw and J. Speirs *Truth and the Child 10 Years On: Information Exchange in Donor Assisted Conception* (Birmingham: British Association of Social Workers, 1998).

E. Blyth (1998) 'Donor assisted conception and donor offspring rights to genetic origin information' *Int. J. Children's Rights* Vol. 6, p. 237. E. Blyth, and J. Hunt, 'Sharing genetic origin information in donor assisted conception. Views from licensed centres on HFEA donor information form' (1998) *Human Reproduction* Vol. 13, p. 3274. J. Carsten, ' "Knowing where you've come from". Ruptures and continuities of time and kinship in narratives of adoption reunions' (2000) *J. Roy. Anthrop. Inst. (N.S.)* p. 687. Donor Conception Support Group of Australia Inc. *Let the Offspring Speak* (Georges Hall, NSW, The DC Support Group of Australia, 1997). S. Golombok, F.M. Maccallum, E. Goodman and M. Rutter 'Families with children conceived by donor insemination: A follow-up at age twelve' (2002) *Child Development* Vol. 73, p. 952. C. Gottlieb, O. Lalos and E. Lindblad, 'Disclosure of donor insemination to the child: the impact of Swedish legislation' (2000) *Human Reproduction* Vol. 15, p. 2052. D. Howe and J. Feast, *Adoption, Search and Reunion*, London, The Children's Society, 2000. S. MacLean and M. MacLean 'Secrets in assisted reproduction – the tension between donor anonymity and the need of the child for information' (1996) *Child and Family Law Quarterly* Vol. 8, p. 243. J. McWinnie *Families Following Assisted Conception. What Do We Tell Our Child?* Dundee, Dept of Law, University of Dundee, 1996. J.S. Modell *Kinship with Strangers. Adoption and Interpretation of Kinship in American Culture*, Berkeley, University of California Press, 1994. K. O'Donovan, 'What shall we tell the children? Reflections on children's perspectives and the reproduction revolution', in R. Lee and D. Morgan (eds) *Birthright, Law and Ethics and the Beginning of Life*, London, Routledge, 1989. O. O'Neill, What is Genetic Identity? (unpublished, 2002). Newnham College, Cambridge. M. Richards, 'Future bodies: Some history and future prospects for human genetic selection', in A. Bainham, S. Day-Sclater and M. Richards (eds), *Body Lore and Laws*, Oxford, Hart Publishing, 2002. M. Richards 'Assisted reproduction and genetic technologies and family life', in J. Scott, J. Treas, and M.P.M. Richards (eds), *Blackwell Companion to the Sociology of Families*, Oxford, Blackwell, 2003. S. Wilson, 'Identity, genealogy and the social family: The case of donor insemination' (1997) *Int. J. Law, Policy & The Family* Vol. 11, p. 270.

27 As most, including the present author, believe they should be.

28 See note 7 above.

29 Cloning will not produce truly identical twins except in this scenario

because of the mitochondrial DNA contained in the egg and derived from the mother of the donated egg.

30 O'Neill op. cit., p. 68.

31 For fun, see the seminal work on ambiguity in literature, William Empson's *Seven Types of Ambiguity*, London: Chatto and Windus 1970.

32 E. Ferr. *Growing Up in a One-Parent Family*, Windsor: NFER Publishing 1976.

33 I leave aside possible further multiplication of genetic parenting where the egg cell contains mitochondrial DNA from a third party.

34 For the sake of brevity I don't now challenge the claim of O'Neill that this would be psychologically damaging. I doubt there exists any compelling evidence, O'Neill certainly produces none – my guess is that this is just a piece of unsupported speculation on O'Neill's part.

35 For further reasons to be sceptical about the precautionary principle, see John Harris and Søren Holm 'Extended lifespan and the paradox of precaution', *The Journal of Medicine and Philosophy* 2002.

36 For detailed philosophical justification of this symmetry between acts and omissions see my *Violence & Responsibility*, Routledge & Kegan Paul 1980.

37 Of course regulating sexual reproduction would be much more complex, costly and difficult. It would also be more problematic in terms of civil liberties.

38 For more on procreative liberty see my 'Genes, clones and human rights' in Justine C. Burley (ed.) *The Genetic Revolution and Human Rights: The Amnesty Lectures 1998*, Oxford: Oxford University Press 1999, pp. 61–95. Ronald Dworkin *Life's Dominion*, London: HarperCollins, 1993, p. 148. See also John A. Robertson *Children of Choice*, Princeton: Princeton University Press, 1994, especially Chapter 2.

39 See my 'Rights and reproductive choice' in John Harris and Søren Holm (eds). *The Future of Human Reproduction: Choice and Regulation*, Oxford: Oxford University Press, 1998, pp. 5–37.

40 See John Harris 'The welfare of the child' in *Health Care Analysis* 2000, pp. 1–8. and also Justine Burley and John Harris 'Human cloning and child welfare' in *The Journal of Medical Ethics* Vol. 25, February 1999.

41 I deliberately repeat O'Neill's use of the term 'would-be' here to confirm that she would regard it as legitimate.

42 D. Parfit *Reasons and Persons*, Oxford: Clarendon Press, 1984, Chapter 16.

43 Burley and Harris, op. cit.

44 Ibid. p. 358.

45 This is Parfit's point made here in the plural. Ibid., p. 359.

46 This term of art is used in The Human Fertilization and Embryology Act 1990. Clause 13.5 of that Act states: 'A woman shall not be provided with treatment services unless account has been taken of the welfare of the child who may be born as a result of the treatment (including the need of that child for a father), and of any other child who may be affected by the birth.' See my 'The welfare of the child' in *Health Care Analysis* 2000, pp. 1–8.

47 See Joel Feinberg 'The child's right to an open future' in his *Freedom and Fulfilment*, Princeton: Princeton University Press, 1992, pp. 76–98.

48 Ibid, p. 80.

49 *Prince v. Massachusetts* 321 US 158 (1944).

50 Ibid. at pp. 168, 170.

51 In this and in the next section I have borrowed some ideas from Katrien Devolder, who has made a detailed study of objections to cloning.

52 S. Holm 'A life in the shadow: One reason why we should not clone humans', *Cambridge Quarterly of Healthcare Ethics* 1998, Vol. 7, pp. 160–162.

53 L.R. Kass 'The wisdom of repugnance', *The New Republic* 1997, p. 23.

54 R. Deech 1999 'Human cloning and public policy' in J. Burley (ed.) *The Genetic Revolution and Human Rights*, Oxford: Oxford University Press, Ch. 4.

FOUR   SAFETY AND DANGER

1 *The Universal Declaration on the Human Genome and Human Rights*, published by UNESCO as a pamphlet 3 December 1997.

2 For more in this see my 'The ethical use of human embryonic stem cells' in *Medicine and Philosophy* Vol. 23, No. 10, October 2002, pp. 6–14. And my 'The use of human embryonic stem cells in research and therapy' in Justine C. Burley and John Harris (eds) *A Companion to Genethics: Philosophy and the Genetic Revolution*, Oxford: Basil Blackwell, 2002, pp. 158–175. See also 'Intimations of immortality – the ethics and justice of life extending therapies' in Michael Freeman (ed.) *Current Legal Problems*, Oxford: Oxford University Press 2002, pp. 65–95.

3 Except by Pedro Lowenstein, who pointed them out to me.

4 These possibilities were pointed out to me by Pedro Lowenstein who is currently working on the implications for human gene therapy.

5 For more on immortality see my 'Intimations of immortality' in *Science* Vol. 288, No. 5463, p. 59, 7 April 2000, and 'Intimations of immortality – the ethics and justice of life extending therapies' in Michael Freeman (ed.) *Current Legal Problems*, Oxford: Oxford University Press 2002, pp. 65–95.

6 Phoenix, London 1998.

7 Ibid., p. 228.

8 Ibid., 232.

9 Ibid., pp. 233–234.

10 For the record this is the incoherent bit! What counts as disequilibrium and when and why might it be bad to unbalance the milieu in a good cause?

11 For a discussion of the rationality of the precautionary principle which Rifkin is employing here see John Harris and Søren Holm 'Extended lifespan and the paradox of precaution' in *The Journal of Medicine and Philosophy* Vol. 27, No. 3, 2002.

12 Jeremy Rifkin 'Cloning: What hath genomics wrought?' *Los Angeles Times*, 3 February 2000.

13 From Common Dreams NewsCenter http://www.commondreams.org/

14 I have been unable to trace the history of this claim by Rifkin. It may be that a patent was initially and erroneously granted by the Patent Office but as will be seen in the discussion that follows, such a patent is now illegal and must have been revoked if it ever existed.

15 Patents Act 1977, Schedule A2, Paragraph 3(a) I am grateful to my colleague David Booton for his invaluable advice on Intellectual Property Law.

16 The ideas in this section, and indeed the way they are treated, result from collaborative work I did with my colleague Simona Giordano. She must take a good share of the credit (or blame) for what appears here. See John Harris and Simona Giordano 'On cloning', *The Routledge Encyclopedia of Philosophy*, Edward Craig (ed.) Online Edition. Publication online 2003.

17 See John Harris *Clones, Genes and Immortality*, Oxford: Oxford University Press, 1998, p. 178.

18 See A. Buchanan, D.W. Brock, N. Daniels and D. Wickler, *From Chance to Choice: Genetics and Justice*, Cambridge: Cambridge University Press, 2000.

19 I have not been able to find citations for this but in my experience of

addressing audiences over many years on the subject of cloning this spectre is often raised.

20 In this section I draw upon arguments developed jointly with Julian Savulescu in Julian Savulescu and John Harris 'The creation lottery', *Cambridge Quarterly of Health Care Ethics*, Vol. 12, No. 1, January 2004, pp. 90–95.

21 'Reprogramming cell fate – transgenesis and cloning', *Reprod. Fertil. Develop.*, Special Issue 1999, Vol. 10, Nos. 7, 8.

22 National Bioethics Advisory Commission, *Cloning Human Beings*, Maryland: National Bioethics Advisory Commission, 1997.

23 I owe this example to Julian Savulescu.

24 Elsewhere Julian Savulescu and I have called both natural procreation and cloning 'creation lotteries' in that 'A creation lottery involves the creation of a population of embryos for the purpose of creating a new human being and this practice involves the unavoidable death of some of these embryos and the unavoidable production of grossly deformed and disabled human beings.' In this respect sexual reproduction and cloning are both most certainly 'creation lotteries'. See note 22 above.

FIVE   THERAPEUTIC CLONING AND STEM CELL RESEARCH AND THERAPY

1 See my 'Stem cells, sex and procreation' in *Cambridge Quarterly of Healthcare Ethics*, Vol. 12, No. 4, Fall 2003, pp. 353–372.

2 While other equally platitudinous but also totally incoherent principles, like the appeal to human dignity, so often occupy centre stage.

3 Or who even believes that unprotected sexual intercourse is permissible.

4 Of course there may be specific research projects that are unethical.

5 John Harris 'Intimations of immortality', *Science*, Vol. 288, No. 5463 7 April 2000, p. 59. John Harris 'Intimations of immortality – The ethics and justice of life extending therapies' in Michael Freeman (ed.) *Current Legal Problems* 2002.

6 And perhaps most religionists too, but that is a different kind of immortality.

7 Tom Kirkwood *Time of our Lives*, Weidenfeld and Nicolson, London, 1999 and *The End of Age*, Profile Books, London, 2001.

8 John Harris 'Intimations of immortality', *Science*, Vol. 288, No. 5463, 7 April 2000; p. 59. John Harris 'Intimations of immortality – The ethics and justice of life extending therapies' in Michael Freeman (ed.) *Current Legal Problems* 2002.

9 For more on the ethics of genetic enhancement see my *Clones, Genes and Immortality* Oxford University Press 1998.

10 And indeed the life sciences more generally.

11 This section was researched and substantially drafted by my colleague Louise Irving; I am grateful to her here as elsewhere for help and advice.

12 Stem Cell Research: Medical Progress with Responsibility, Department of Health June 2000. Government Response to the Recommendations made in the Chief Medical Officer's Expert Group Report 'Stem Cell Research: Medical Progress with Responsibility. Presented to Parliament by the Secretary of State For Health By Command of Her Majesty August 2000. The Stationery Office Cm 4833.

13 And also an unsupportable claim unless the immorality consists solely in the fact that as yet cloning by cell nuclear transfer is untested and probable unsafe in humans.

14 This is the case in France, Germany, Ireland, Lithuania and Switzerland.

15 This has been legal in the UK since the 1990 Human Fertilisation and Embryology Authority Act came into force.

16 The 8th Amendment of the Constitution Act 1983 reads 'acknowledged the right to life of the unborn, with due regard to the equal right of the mother' – 7 October 1983 in *Constitution of Ireland* at http://www.irlgov.ie/taoiseach/publication/constitution/english/contents.htm.

17 Marcin Frydrych 'Abortion not considered in enlargement rules' at http://www.euobserver.com/index.phtml?aid-4646.

18 From: The Opinion of the European Group on Ethics in Science and New Technologies to the European Commission, No. 15, 14 November 2000, *Ethical Aspects of Stem Cell Research and Use*, p. 11

19 Spanish regulation is through the Assisted Reproduction Techniques Act of 1988, taken from the Spanish Survey on Human Embryonic Stem Cells in the European Commission Research Directorate-General *Survey on Opinions from National Ethics Committees or Similar Bodies Public Debate and*

National Legislation in relation to Human Embryonic Stem Cell Research and Use, edited by Line Matthiessen November 2001.

20 See Robert P. Lanza et al. 'The ethical validity of using nuclear transfer in human transplantation', JAMA 27 December 2000, Vol. 284, No. 24, p. 3175.

21 From The Convention of the Protection of Human Rights and Dignity of the Human Being with regard to the Application of Biology and Medicine: Convention on Human Rights and Biomedicine, which states: (1) Where the law allows research on embryos *in vitro,* it shall ensure adequate protection of the embryo; (2) The creation of embryos for research purposes is prohibited.

22 The Charter of the Fundamental Rights of the European Union can be found on http://ue.eu.int/df/docs/en/CharteEN.pdf.

23 The European Group of Ethics in Science and New Technologies to the European Commission website can be found at http://europa.eu.int/comm/european_group_ethics/index_en.htm

24 Taken from http://news.bbc.co.uk/hi/english/world/europe/newsid 'German bishop capitulates on abortion'.

25 *Maranatha Christian Journal* at http://www.mcjonline.com/news/news3219.htm

26 Statement of the Central Ethics Committee on Stem Cell Research 23.11.01 (non-official translation) annexe of The European Commission Research Directorate-General, *Survey on Opinions from National Ethics Committees or Similar Bodies Public Debate and National Legislation in relation to Human Embryonic Stem Cell Research and Use,* edited by Line Matthiessen November 2001.

27 From *Nature* 7 Feb. 2002, pp. 415, 566. See also Thomas Heinemann and Ludger Honnefelder 'Principles of ethical decision making regarding embryonic stem cell research' in *Bioethics,* Vol. 16, No. 6 2002.

28 Opinion on the preliminary draft revision of the laws on bioethics of the Comité Consultatif National d'Ethique pour les Sciences – CCNE, in the *Survey of Opinions from National Ethics Committees or similar bodies, public debate and national legislation in relation to human embryonic stem cell research and use,* by the European Commission Research Directorate-General, edited by Line Matthiessen.

29 Ibid.

30 Ibid.

31 Inez de Beaufort and Veronica English 'Between pragmatism and principles? On the morality of using the results of research that a country considers immoral' in J. Gunning (ed.) *Assisted Conception Research, Ethics and Law*, Dartmouth Publishing, Aldershot 2000; and also Ronald M. Green, 'Benefiting from evil, an incipient moral problem in human stem cell research and therapy' in *Bioethics* Vol. 16, No. 6 2002.

32 The Italian National Bioethics document in the *Survey of Opinions from National Ethics Committees or similar bodies, public debate and national legislation in relation to human embryonic stem cell research and use*, by the European Commission Research Directorate-General, edited by Line Matthiessen.

33 Ibid.

34 In my *Wonderwoman and Superman: The Ethics of Human Biotechnology*, Oxford University Press 1992, and its successor volume *Clones, Genes and Immortality*, Oxford University Press 1998.

35 C.M. Verfaillie et al. 'Multipotent adult progenitor cells from bone marrow differentiate into functional hepatocyte-like cells', *J. Clin. Invest.* Vol. 109, pp. 1291–1302, 2002, and 'Pluripotent nature of adult marrow derived mesenchymal stem cells', *Nature* Vol. 418, pp. 41–49, 2002, and C.M. Verfaillie 'Adult stem cells: A case for pluripotency?' *Trends in Cell Biol.* Vol. 12, pp. 502–508, 2002.

36 *International Herald Tribune* 22–23 June 2002, p. 1. Austin Smith has emphasised the importance of pursuing research on all sources of stem cells simultaneously (paper presented at FENS forum Workshop, Paris, 13 July 2002).

37 Roger Pedersen in discussion of his paper 'Embryonic steps towards stem cell medicine' presented at the EUROSTEM Conference *Regulation and Legislation Under Conditions of Scientific Uncertainty*, Bilbao, Spain 6–9 March 2002. The conference was supported by a project grant from the European Commission Directorate-General for Research, 'Quality of Life'.

38 The lessons I draw here have been challenged by Julian Savulescu. See our exchange entitled 'The Great Debates' in *The Cambridge Quarterly of Healthcare Ethics* (2004), Vol. 12, pp. 68–95.

39 Robert Winston gave the figure of five embryos for every live birth some years ago in a personal communication. Anecdotal evidence to me from a number of sources confirms this high figure but the literature is rather more conservative making more probable a figure of three embryos lost for every live birth. See Charles E. Boklage 'Survival

probability of human conceptions from fertilization to term' in *International Journal of Fertility*, Vol. 35, No. 2 1990, pp. 75–94. Also Henri Leridon *Human Fertility: The Basic Components*, University of Chicago Press, Chicago 1977. Again, in a recent personal communication Henri Leridon confirmed that a figure of three lost embryos for every live birth is a reasonable conservative figure.

40 For a conclusive refutation of that doctrine see John Harris *Violence & Responsibility* Routledge and Kegan Paul 1980. For a more recent discussion of these broad issues see F.H. Kamm 'The doctrine of triple effect and why a rational agent need not intend the means to his end'; and John Harris 'The moral difference between throwing a trolley at a person and throwing a person at a trolley. A reply to Francis Kamm' in The Proceedings of the Aristotelian Society 2000.

41 Some hedonistic utilitarians for example.

42 Human monozygotic twinning occurs in roughly one per 270 births (three per 1,000). I take this figure of the rate of natural twinning from Keith L. Moore and T.V.N. Persaud *The Developing Human* (5th edn), W.B. Saunders, Philadelphia, 1993. The rate mentioned there is per 270 pregnancies.

43 Or indeed cloning by cell nuclear substitution, but that is another story. For the full story see my 'Goodbye Dolly: The ethics of human cloning' in *The Journal of Medical Ethics*, Vol. 23, No.6, December 1997, pp. 353–360.

44 The possible objection was put to me by Julian Savulescu – the response to it with all its defects is mine.

45 A point made to me by Louis G. Aldrich at the Third International Conference of Bioethics, National Central University, Shungli, Taiwan 24–29 June 2002.

46 Pub.L.105–277. Section 511, Oct. 21, 1998, Slip Copy. 1998 H.R. 4328.

47 See John Harris: 'Should we experiment on embryos?' in Robert Lee and Derek Morgan (eds) *Birthrights: Law and Ethics at the Beginnings of Life*, London: Routledge 1988, pp. 85–95.

This is an abbreviated selected bibliography. For complete cloning bibliography see http://www.philosophyarena.com/philosophyarena/homepage.htm

Books

Andrews, L.B., *The Clone Age: Adventures in the New World of Reproductive Technology*. New York: Henry Holt and Company, 1999.

Andrews, L.B. and Nelkin, D., *Body Bazaar: The Market for Human Tissue in the Biotechnology Age*. New York: Crown Publications, 2001.

Austad, S.N., *Why We Age: What Science Is Discovering About the Body's Journey Through Life*. New York: Wiley & Sons, Inc., 1997.

Baker, R., *Sex in the Future: Ancient Urges Meet Future Technology*. London: Macmillan, 1999.

Beauchamp, T.L. and Walters, L.R., *Contemporary Issues in Bioethics*. (6th ed.). London: Thomson Corporation, 2003.

Beller, F.K. and Weir, R.F., *The Beginning of Human Life*. Dordrecht: Kluwer Academic Publishers, 1994.

Bonnicksen, A.L., *Crafting a Cloning Policy: From Dolly to Stem Cells*. Washington, DC: Georgetown University Press, 2002.

Brannigan, M.C., ed., *Ethical Issues in Human Cloning: Cross-disciplinary Perspectives*. New York/London: Chatham House, 2001.

Bruce, D., *Cloning – a step too far?* Edinburgh: Society, Religion and Technology, 1997.

Burley, J., ed., *The Genetic Revolution and Human Rights*. Oxford: Oxford University Press, 1999.

Burley, J. and Harris, J., eds, *A Companion to Genethics: Philosophy and the Genetic Revolution*. Oxford: Blackwell, 2002.

Caplan, A.L., *Due Consideration*. New York: Wiley & Sons, Inc., 1997.

Caplan, A.L., *Am I My Brother's Keeper?* Bloomington: Indiana University Press, 1998.

Caplan, A.L., McGee, G. and Anchor, J., 'Ethical Issues in Oocyte and Embryo Donation'. In Sauer, M.V., ed, *Principles of Oocyte and Embryo Donation*. New York: Springer Verlag, 1998: 229–40.

Cohen, D., *Cloning*. Brookfield, CT: Millbrook Press, 1998.

Cole-Turner, R., ed., *Human Cloning, Religious Responses*. Kentucky: John Knox Press, 1997.

Cole-Turner, R., ed., *Beyond Cloning: Religion and the Remaking of Humanity*. Harrisburg, PA: Trinity Press International, 2001.

Committee on Biological, Biomedical Application (ed.), National Research Council, *Stem Cells and the Future of Regenerative Medicine*. National Academy Press, 2002.

Council of Europe, *Ethical Eye: Cloning*. Council of Europe, 2003.

Curran, B., *A Terrible Beauty is Born: Clones, Genes and the Future of Mankind*. London: Taylor & Francis, 2003.

Daniel, P.P., *Human Cloning*. Mall Publishing, 2003.

Dann, J. and Gardner, D., eds, *Clones, Nine Tales of Genetic Engineering and its Impact on Tomorrow*. New York: Ace Books, 1997.

Devolder, K. and Braeckman, J., Copyright. Een bio-ethisch essay. Leuven: Leuven University Press, 2001.

Dudley, W., *The Ethics of Human Cloning*. San Diego, CA: Greenhaven Press, 2001.

Dworkin, R., *Life's Dominion: An Argument About Abortion, Euthanasia, and Individual freedom*. New York: Vintage, 1994.

Dyson, A. and Harris, J., eds, *Experiments on Embryos*. London: Routledge, 1990.

Editors of Scientific American, *Understanding Cloning*. New York: Warner Books, 2002.

Engelhardt, T.H., Jr., *The Foundations of Christian Bioethics*. Lisse, Netherlands: Swets & Zeitlinger, 2000.

Faden, R.R. and Beauchamp, T.L., *A History and Theory of Informed Consent*. New York: Oxford University Press, 1986.

Fotion, N. and Heller, J.C., eds, *Contingent Future Persons. On the Ethics of Deciding Who Will Live, or Not, in the Future*. Dordrecht: Kluwer Academic Publishers, 1997.

Friele, M.B., ed., *Embryo Experimentation in Europe: Biomedical, Legal and Philosophical Aspects*. Bad Neuenahr-Ahrweiler: Graue Reihe, 2001.

Fritz, S., (compiler), Scientific American (ed.), Haseltine, E.W., *Understanding Cloning*. New York: Warner Books, 2002.

Fritz, S., *Genomics and Cloning*. Smart Apple Media, 2003.

Fukuyama, F., *Our Posthuman Future. Consequences of the Biotechnology Revolution*. New York: Farrar, Straus and Giroux, 2002.

Goodnough, D., *The Debate over Human Cloning: A Pro/Con Issue*. Enslow Publishers, Inc., 2003.

Gosden, R., *Designer Babies: The Brave New World of Reproductive Technology*. London: Victor Gollancz, 1999.

Green, R.M., *The Human Embryo Research Debates: Bioethics in the Vortex of Controversy*. Oxford, New York: Oxford University Press, 2001.

Holland, S., Lebacqz, K. and Zoloth, L., eds, *The Human Embryonic Stem Cell Debate. Science, Ethics, and Public Policy*. Cambridge/Massachusetts: The MIT Press, 2001.

Houdebine, L.-M., *Animal Transgenesis and Cloning*. John Wiley & Sons, 2003.

Humber, J. and Almeder, R., eds, *Human Cloning: Biomedical Ethical Reviews*. New Jersey: Humana Press, 1998.

Jonas, H., *The Imperative of Responsibility: In Search of an Ethics For the Technological Age*. Chicago: University of Chicago Press, 1984.

Kass, L.R. and Wilson, J.Q., *The Ethics of Human Cloning*. Washington DC: American Enterprise Institute, 1998.

Kass, L.R., *Human Cloning and Human Dignity: The Report of the President's Council on Bioethics*. PublicAffairs, 2002.

Kevles, D., *In the Name of Eugenics. Genetics and the Uses of Human Heredity*. New York: Harvard University Press, 1995.

Kimbrell, A. and Nathanson, B., *The Human Body Shop : The Cloning, Engineering, and Marketing of Life* (2nd ed.). Washington, DC: Regnery Publishing, Inc., 1998.

Klotzko, A., ed., *Cloning issue. Cambridge Quarterly of Healthcare Ethics*. Cambridge: Cambridge University Press, 1998.

Klotzko, A.J., ed., *The Cloning Sourcebook*. Oxford: Oxford University Press, 2001.

Kuhse, H. and Singer, P., *Individuals, Humans, Persons: Questions of Life and Death*. Sankt Augustin: Academia Verlag, 1994.

Kuhse, H. and Singer, P., eds, *Bioethics: An Anthology*. Oxford: Blackwell Publishers Ltd, 1999.

Kunich, J.C., *The Naked Clone: How Cloning Bans Threaten Our Personal Rights*. Praeger Publishers, 2003.

Lauritzen, P., ed., *Cloning and the Future of Human Embryo Research*. Oxford/New York: Oxford University Press, 2001.

Lebacqz, K., Holland, S. and Zoloth, L., eds, *Immortal Cells/Mortal Selves*. Bloomington: Indiana University Press, 2001.

MacKinnon, B., ed., *Human Cloning: Science, Ethics, and Public Policy*. Urbana, Chicago: University of Illinois Press, 2000.

Maienschein, J., *Whose View of Life?: Embryos, Cloning, and Stem Cells*. Harvard University Press, 2003.

Marlin, G., *The Politician's Guide to Assisted Suicide, Cloning and Other Current Controversies*. Washington DC: Morley Books, 1998.

McCeun, G., ed., *Cloning, Science & Society, Ideas in Conflict*. Hudson: Gary E. McCuen, 1998.

McGee, G., ed., *Pragmatic Bioethics*. Nashville: Vanderbilt University Press, 1998.

McGee, G., ed., *The Human Cloning Debate* (2nd ed). Berkeley, CA: Berkeley Hills Books, 2000.

McGee, G., *The Perfect Baby: Parenthood in the New World of Cloning and Genetics*. Lanham MD: Rowman & Littlefield, 2000.

Mulkay, M., *The Embryo Research Debate*. Cambridge: Cambridge University Press, 1997.

Nardo, D., *Cloning*. Blackbirch Marketing, 2003. (age: 9–12).

Neri, D., *La Bioetica in Laboratorio*, Roma-Bari: Laterza, 2001.

Nussbaum, M.C. and Sunstein, C.R., eds, *Clones and Clones: Facts and fantasies About Human Cloning*. New York: W. W. Norton and Company, 1998.

Oderberg, D., *Moral theory: A Non-consequentialist Approach*. Oxford: Blackwell, 2000.

Oderberg, D., *Applied ethics: A Non-consequentialist Approach*. Oxford: Blackwell, 2000.

O'Neill, O., *Autonomy and Trust in Bioethics*. Cambridge: Cambridge University Press, 2001.

Parens, E., *Enhancing Human Traits: Ethical and Social Implications*. Washington, DC: Georgetown University Press, 2000.

Parfit, D., *Reasons and Persons*. New York: Oxford University Press, 1984.

Pence, G.E., ed., *Flesh of My Flesh: The Ethics of Cloning Humans, A Reader*. Lanham, MD/Oxford: Rowman and Littlefield, 1998.

Pence, G.E., *Who's Afraid of Human Cloning*. Lanham, MD/Oxford: Rowman & Littlefield Publishers, Inc., 1998.

Pence, G.E., *Classic Cases in Medical Ethics* (3rd ed.). USA: McGraw-Hill, 2002.

Peters, T., *For the Love of Children*. Louisville, KY: Westminster/John Know Press, 1996.

Potten, C.S., ed., *Stem Cells*. London/San Diego: Academic Press, 1997.

Prentice, D.A. and Palladino, M.A., *Stem Cells and Cloning*. Benjamin/Cummings, 2002.

Quesenberry, P.J., Stein, G. and Forget, B., *Stem Cell Biology and Gene Therapy*. New York: John Wiley & Sons, 1998.

Ramsey, P., *Fabricated Man: The Ethics of Genetic Control*. New Haven, CT: Yale University Press, 1970.

Rantala, M.L. and Milgram, A.J., eds, *Cloning: For and Against*. Chicago, IL.: Open Court Publishing Company, 1998.

Ridley, M., *Nature Via Nurture: Genes, Experience and What makes Us Human*. London. Fourth Estate, 2003.

Ruse, M. and Sheppard, A., eds, *Cloning: Responsible Science or Technomadness?* New York: Prometheus Books, 2001.

Ruse, M. and Pynes, C., eds, *The Stem Cell Controversy: Debating the Issues*. Amherst, NY: Prometheus Books, 2002.

Scharper, S.B., *Spiritual Perspectives on Biotechnology: Cloning, Genomes, Cell Research & the Value of Human Life*. Woodstock, VT: Skylight Paths Publishing, 2004.

Segal, N., *Entwined Lives: Twins and What They Tell Us About Human Behavior*. New York: Dutton, 1999.

Shostak, S., *Becoming Immortal: Combining Cloning and Stem-Cell Therapy*. New York: State University of New York, 2002.

Silver, L.M., *Remaking Eden: Cloning and Beyond in a Brave New World*. New York: Avon Books, Inc., 1997.

Singer, P., Kuhse, H., Buckle, S., Dawson, K. and Kasimba, P., *Embryo Experimentation: Ethical, Legal, and Social Issues*. New York: Cambridge University Press, 1990.

Steinbock, B., *Life Before Birth: The Moral and Legal Status of Embryos and Fetuses*. New York: Oxford University Press, 1992.

Stock, G., *Redesigning Humans: Our Inevitable Genetic Future*. Boston, Massachusetts: Houghton Mifflin Company, 2003.

US Government, *21st Century Complete Guide to Human Cloning – Federal Government Information from Congress, FDA, NOH, and the White House, Bioethics and Legal Implications, Legislation and Congressional Testimony, Future of Medicine and Genetics, Human Case Studies, Inside the Cell*. CD-ROM. Progressive Management, 2003.

Warnock, M., *Making Babies: Is There a Right to Have Children?*, Oxford: Oxford University Press, 2002.

Warren, M.A., *Moral Status: Obligations of Persons and Other Living Things*. Oxford: Clarendon Press, 1997.

Water, B., Cole-Turner, R., eds, *God and the Embryo: Religious Perspectives on Stem Cells and Cloning*. Georgetown University Press, 2003.

West, M., *The Immortal Cell: How Stem Cell Biotechnology Can Conquer Cancer and Extend Life*. Doubleday, 2003.

Wilmut, I., Campbell, K. and Tudge, C., *The Second Creation: Dolly and the Age of Biological Control*. London: Headline Book Publishing, 2000.

Winters, P.A., ed., *Cloning*. San Diego, CA: Greenhaven Press, 1998.

Wright, L., *Twins, Genes, Environment and the Mystery of Identity*. London: Weidenfeld & Nicolson, 1997.

Cloning and stem cells websites

American Association for the Advancement of Science. Center for Science, Technology, and Congress. AAAS Policy Brief: Stem Cell Research.
http://www.aaas.org/spp/cstc/briefs/stemcells/index.shtml.

American Journal of Bioethics. Links to Stem cell research and Cloning:
http://www.bioethics.net/resources/index.php?t=display_link_search&having=32296&cat=

Bioethics Today (brings together ethical, medical, legal, social science and lay perspectives on biomedical research and biotechnology related to animals, humans and agriculture. Links to articles on cloning and stem cell research). http://www.bioethics-today.org.

BioSpace: latest news on cloning:
http://www.biospace.com/b2/whats_new/dolly.cfm.

CaringForKinsey.Com (information on the Kinsey Morrison case):
http://caringforkinsey.com/.

Center for Bioethics and Human Dignity. Stem Cell Research.
http://www.cbhd.org/resources/stemcells/.

Centre for Law and Genetics (Australia): Stem Cells.
http://lawgenecentre.org/stemcells?PHPSESSID=6359675ef538dc1204a4e155f4d43df7.

Cloning timeline:
http://atheism.about.com/library/chronologies/blchron_sci_cloning.htm.

CNN in dept special on stem cell research:
http://www.cnn.com/SPECIALS/2001/stemcell/.

Conceiving a clone. Provides a timeline of cloning and biotechnology break-throughs, explanations and animations of various cloning techniques, and scientist biographies, and views on both sides of the cloning debate: http://library.thinkquest.org/24355/.

Council of Europe Steering Committee on Bioethics (CDBI): Links to reports, and stem cell & cloning websites:

http://www.coe.int/T/E/Legal_affairs/Legal_co-operation/Bioethics/.

Cryo-Cell. Info on private cord blood banking:

http://www.cryoc.com/en/index.html.

Do No Harm: The Coalition of Americans for Research Ethics:

http://www.stemcellresearch.org.

European Commission. Links to help understand the stem cells debate: http://europa.eu.int/comm/research/quality-of-life/stemcells/links.html.

Ferti Net, worldwide fertility network. Info on fertility related issues and treatments: http://www.ferti.net/.

Genome News Network. Stem Cell Alert: Law and Players. By M. Garfinkel: http://www.genomenewsnetwork.org/articles/05_03/stem_sec.shtml.

Geron Corporation. Stem Cell Area. Registry, protocols, scientific bibliography: http://www.geron.com.

Globalchange: Cloning news: http://globalchange.com/clonlink.htm.

Human Cloning Foundation. The official web site of the Human Cloning Foundation (US), has links to articles in support of human cloning as well as links to resources, news and discussion groups:

http://www.humancloning.org/.

McGee G. Primer on Ethics and Human Cloning. Interesting links to other websites and articles:

http://www.actionbioscience.org/biotech/mcgee.html.

Medline plus Health Information: Stem Cells/Stem Cell Transplantation: Latest news and inks to related websites:

http://www.nlm.nih.gov/medlineplus/stemcellsstemcelltransplantation.html.

National Institute of Health. NIH Stem Cell Information:

http://www.nih.gov/news/stemcell/index.htm.

New Scientist. Articles on cloning and stem cells, and links to other relevant sites: http://www.newscientist.com/hottopics/cloning/.

Pecorino L. *Stem Cells for Cell-Based Therapies*. An actionbioscience.org original article with links to other stem cells websites and articles:

http://www.actionbioscience.org/biotech/pecorino2.html.

PhRMA Genomics: cloning & stem cell research. Site provided by Pharmaceutical Research and Manufacturers of America with links to the latest news stories, resources and US congressional activities:

http://genomics.phrma.org/cloning.html.

Roslin Institute Online. Background material and press releases concerning the cloning research conducted at the Institute:

http://www.roslin.ac.uk/public/cloning.html.

SFClone. Clone: movies, TV-movies, fiction about cloning, genetic engineering, and human duplication:

http://www.magicdragon.com/UltimateSF/clone.html#clone-movies.

Stem Cells: International Journal of Cell Differentiation and Proliferation:

http://stemcells.alphamedpress.org/.

Stem Cell Research Foundation:

http://www.stemcellresearchfoundation.org/About/about.htm.

Stem Cell Research News: http://www.stemcellresearchnews.com/. !!!

University of Wisconsin: news and background information detailing embryonic stem cell research at the University of Wisconsin-Madison.:

http://www.news.wisc.edu/packages/stemcells/.

White House, Pres. George W. Bush. Links to stem cells and cloning news releases.: http://www.whitehouse.gov/.

Yahoo directory of useful web sites on cloning:

http://dir.yahoo.com/Science/Biology/Genetics/Cloning/.

Films about cloning and human duplication (with critical comments taken from http://www.magicdragon.com/UltimateSF/clone.html)

Anna to the Infinite Power (1983): An under-rated film starring Martha Byrne as the troubled child prodigy Anna, whose quest for identity leads in an unexpected direction. There's a tie-in to the holocaust here, in a substantially different direction than *The Boys from Brazil*.

Blade Runner (1982): The modern classic based on Philip K. Dick's novel 'Do Androids Dream of Electric Sheep'. That title has an extra irony now, with the cloning of 'Dolly' – a sheep, as the first clone of an adult mammal. The film stars Harrison Ford, Rutger Hauer and Sean Young. The Director's Cut is the recommended version.

The Boys from Brazil (1978): From the Ira Levin novel, this shows the darkest side of cloning humans: it might be evil and powerful men like Hitler that get genetically duplicated.

Critters (1986): Extraterrestrials have the technology, and use it to overwhelm humanity with furry creatures somewhat less benign than 'tribbles'.

The Human Duplicators (1965): Extraterrestrials start copying and replacing people in this routine sci-fi thriller.

Il Gatto a nove code (1970): Cats are experimented upon in this film, and it leads to something stranger than merely 'nine lives'.

The Island of Dr Moreau (1977): This is the original film adaptation of the 1896 H.G. Wells novel, starring Burt Lancaster, Michael York, Richard Basehart and Barbara Carrera.

The Island of Dr Moreau (1996): This is the remake of the H.G. Wells 1896 novel, starring Marlon Brando, Val Kilmer and Ron Perlman. A big budget and great cast wasted.

It Came from Outer Space II (1996): A weak sequel, with aliens duplicating humans for nefarious purposes.

Man's Best Friend (1993): This film centres on genetic engineering of dogs. It is blatantly ripped off from the wonderful novel 'Sirius' by Olaf Stapledon. Why not make a film of that novel, instead?

Multiplicity (1996): The acting and special effects are good, which disguises a screenplay filled with holes, and an opportunity for deeper comedy and philosophy wasted.

Night of the Lepus (1972): Killer rabbits. Need I say more?

The Resurrection of Zachary Wheeler (1971): Not a bad film on this subject, basically ahead of its time.

Previous publications by John Harris relevant to cloning

In writing this book I have consciously (and doubtless sometimes unconsciously) drawn on these previous writings on cloning.

Books

1. *The Value of Life*, Routledge & Kegan Paul, 1985.
2. *Clones, Genes and Immortality*, Oxford University Press, 1998. (This is an updated and revised new edition of my *Wonderwoman and Superman*, Oxford University Press 1992.)

3. John Harris and Søren Holm (eds), *The Future of Human Reproduction*, Clarendon Press, Oxford, 1998.

Papers in refereed academic journals (published or in press)

1. '*In vitro* fertilisation: the ethical issues' in *The Philosophical Quarterly* Vol. 33, No. 132, July 1983.
2. 'Goodbye Dolly: The ethics of human cloning' in *The Journal of Medical Ethics* Vol. 23, No. 6, December 1997, pp. 353–360.
3. 'Cloning and human dignity' in *Cambridge Quarterly of Healthcare Ethics*, Spring, 1998, Vol. 7, No. 2, pp. 163–168.
4. 'Ethics and Cloning' in *Zeitschrift für Philosophie* Vol. 1, No. 2, January 1999.
5. Justine Burley and John Harris 'Human cloning and child welfare' in *The Journal of Medical Ethics* Vol. 25, February 1999.
6. 'The concept of the person and the value of life' in *Kennedy Institute of Ethics Journal* Vol. 9, No. 4, 1999, pp. 293–308.
7. 'Clones, genes and reproductive autonomy' in Raphael Cohen-Almagor (ed.). *Medical Ethics at the Dawn of the 21st Century*, Annals of the New York Academy of Sciences, Vol. 913, September 2000, pp. 209–218.
8. 'The welfare of the child' in *Health Care Analysis* 2000, pp. 1–8.
9. 'Intimations of immortality' in *Science* Vol. 288, No. 5463, 7 April 2000, p. 59.
10. 'The ethical use of human embryonic stem cells' in *The Journal of Medicine and Philosophy* Vol. 23, No. 10, October 2002, pp. 6–14.
11. 'Is cloning an attack on human dignity?' in *Nature* Vol. 387, 20 June 1997, p. 754.
12. 'Cloning and bioethical thinking' in *Nature* Vol. 389, 2 October 1997, p. 433.
13. Simona Giordano and John Harris, 'Bioetica e tecnologia, medica. Clonazione, ricerca sulle cellule staminali, statuto morale degli embrioni' in *Bioetica* 3/2003, pp. 427–441.
14. Fabio Bacchini and John Harris 'Being positive about positive genetic manipulation' in *Medicina nei secoli: Arte e scienza* (Journal of History of Medicine) Vol. 15, No. 1, 2003, pp. 17–35.
15. 'Stem cells, sex and procreation', in *Cambridge Quarterly of Healthcare Ethics* Vol. 12, No. 4, Fall 2003, pp. 353–372.

16. 'The Great Debates – Julian Savulescu and John Harris' in *Cambridge Quarterly of Healthcare Ethics* Vol. 13, No. 1, January 2004, pp. 68–96. My contributions to this debate: 'Sexual reproduction is a survival lottery' pp. 75–90.

17. Julian Savulescu and John Harris 'The creation lottery: final lessons from natural reproduction: why those who accept natural reproduction should accept cloning and other Frankenstein reproductive technologies' in *Cambridge Quarterly of Healthcare Ethics* Vol. 13, No. 1, January 2004, pp. 90–96.

Book chapters and essays in symposia (published or in press)

1. 'Rights and reproductive choice' in John Harris and Søren Holm (eds). *The Future of Human Reproduction: Choice and Regulation*, Oxford, University Press, 1998, pp. 5–37.

2. 'Genes, clones and human rights' in Justine C. Burley (ed.). *The Genetic Revolution and Human Rights: The Amnesty Lectures 1998*, Oxford University Press, Oxford, 1999, pp. 61–95.

3. 'Cloning and balanced ethics' in Iain Torrance (ed.). *Bioethics in the New Millennium*, St Andrews Press, St Andrews, 2000.

4. 'The scope and importance of bioethics' in John Harris (ed.). *Bioethics, Oxford Readings in Philosophy*, Oxford University Press, 2001, pp. 1–22.

5. 'The use of human embryonic stem cells in research and therapy' in Justine C. Burley and John Harris (eds). *A Companion to Genethics: Philosophy and the Genetic Revolution*, Oxford: Basil Blackwell, 2002, pp. 158–175.

6. 'Intimations of immortality – the ethics and justice of life extending therapies' in Michael Freeman (ed.). *Current Legal Problems*, Oxford University Press, 2002, pp. 65–95.

7. 'Cloning' in R.G. Frey and Kit Wellman (eds). *The Blackwells Companion to Applied Ethics*, Basil Blackwell, Oxford, 2003.

8. 'Reproductive Choice' in *Encyclopaedia of the Human Genome*, London: Nature Publishing Group Reference Publication 2003.

9. John Harris, Derek Morgan and Mary Ford 'Stem cells: Ethics and regulation' in *The Encyclopaedia of Bioethics*, Macmillan (in press).

10. John Harris and Simona Giordano 'On cloning', *The Routledge Encyclopaedia of Philosophy* (ed.). Edward Craig, Routledge On Line, 2003.

Other publications (reports, letters, professional journal articles, etc.)

1. 'Demi-gods and mortals' in *The Independent on Sunday*, 16 January 2000.
2. 'Legislation has no place in the cloning debate' in *The Independent*, 21 September 2000.
3. 'Genetic information and the unexamined life', Personal view in *The BMJ* Vol. 322, 28 April 2001, p. 1070.
4. 'Human reproductive cloning', cover feature in *The Fabian Review* Vol. 115, No. 1, Spring 2003, pp. 14–15.

Index

THINKING IN ACTION – order more now

Available from all good bookshops

Credit card orders can be made on our **Customer Hotlines**:
UK/RoW: + (0) 8700 768 853
US/Canada: (1) 800 634 7064

Or buy online at: www.routledge.com

Routledge
Taylor & Francis Group

Title	Author	Isbn	Bind	Prices UK	US	Canada
On Belief	Slavoj Zizek	0415255325	PB	£8.99	$14.95	$19.95
On Cosmopolitanism and Forgiveness	Jacques Derrida	0415227127	PB	£8.99	$14.95	$19.95
On Film	Stephen Mulhall	0415247969	PB	£8.99	$14.95	$19.95
On Being Authentic	Charles Guignon	0415261236	PB	£8.99	$14.95	$19.95
On Humour	Simon Critchley	0415251214	PB	£8.99	$14.95	$19.95
On Immigration and Refugees	Sir Michael Dummett	0415227089	PB	£8.99	$14.95	$19.95
On Anxiety	Renata Salecl	0415312760	PB	£8.99	$14.95	$19.95
On Literature	Hillis Miller	0415261252	PB	£8.99	$14.95	$19.95
On Religion	John D Caputo	041523333X	PB	£8.99	$14.95	$19.95
On Humanism	Richard Norman	0415305233	PB	£8.99	$14.95	$19.95
On Science	Brian Ridley	0415249805	PB	£8.99	$14.95	$19.95
On Stories	Richard Kearney	0415247985	PB	£8.99	$14.95	$19.95
On Personality	Peter Goldie	0415305144	PB	£8.99	$14.95	$19.95
On the Internet	Hubert Dreyfus	0415228077	PB	£8.99	$14.95	$19.95
On Evil	Adam Morton	0415305195	PB	£8.99	$14.95	$19.95
On the Meaning of Life	John Cottingham	0415248000	PB	£8.99	$14.95	$19.95
On Cloning	John Harris	0415317002	PB	£8.99	$14.95	$19.95

Contact our **Customer Hotlines** for details of postage
and packing charges where applicable.
All prices are subject to change
without notification.

...Big ideas to fit in your pocket